Praise for 10 Life-Charged Words

Deftly interweaving poignant stories, cutting insight, and pastoral sensitivity, Maul names and addresses important questions for men as they explore faith beyond the surface. Unlike many other authors who frame men's issues in reaction to the issues of women, Maul attempts to get at core struggles and possibilities that are present in the life of men. This approach does not create a false dichotomy between men and women or a posture of scarcity of God's call on humanity; rather Maul gives an opportunity for men to be the people of faith that God has called each of them to be.

REV. BRUCE REYES-CHOW
Blogger and Moderator of the 218th
General Assembly of the Presbyterian Church (USA)

Derek Maul reminds us that the God of the universe who spoke this world into being is still speaking today—and as Derek writes, "Jesus wants in on the conversation of our day-to-day lives." *10 Life-Charged Words* is a passionate encouragement to let the living power of the Word give new life to our own words and lives, never losing sight of the source of that power—our daily walk and our daily conversation with Jesus.

GREGG HUBBARD
Keyboardist/vocalist for Sawyer Brown

I have worked with Derek for years and found him to be one of the most engaging writers for men I have ever known. This latest work does not disappoint. This is a spiritual feast for men that will literally change their lives.

BRYAN DAVIS
Director of All Pro Dad
Family First

Derek Maul is a deep breath of fresh air for Christian men all over the world. He is unashamedly and uncompromisingly an agitator and activist for Christ. His passion when speaking on the topic of Christian men and their role in the church and everyday society is inspiring. It is a timely call to arms for Christian men as individuals and as Christian men's groups to become what Jesus needs—passionate, energetic soldiers and practitioners of the Gospel of Love. This book is a worthy successor to his previous title *Get Real.*

ROLAND RINK
The Upper Room, South Africa

Derek Maul knows men! He understands what makes us tick, what our excuses are, and where our passions lie. These words of spirituality and religion will hold us accountable, inspire us, and help us form even deeper in the love of Christ.

He brings to us words from the vocabulary of culture and helps us look beneath the words, inside the words, and around the words to see the spiritual meaning of each. His openness and honesty will disarm you and lead you to a strengthened faith experience.

BO PROSSER, Coordinator for Missional Congregations
Cooperative Baptist Fellowship

Inspirational writer Derek Maul challenges men that "God wants us to drop the religion and embrace a spirituality that is charged with abundant life." His choice of ten life-charged words facilitates that forward moving journey. Grasp them and live the life.

DAVE ANDREWS is a men's leader
in the Baptist Union of Great Britain

10

LIFE-CHARGED

WORDS

REAL FAITH FOR MEN

DEREK MAUL

UPPER
ROOM BOOKS®
NASHVILLE

The Upper Room Web site: www.upperroom.org

The definitions at the beginning of each chapter are a hybridization of the author's ideas and other sources. In several cases, names, characters, and events are either the products of the author's imagination or used in a fictitious manner to protect the anonymity and privacy of individuals. Any resemblance to actual persons, living or dead, or actual events is purely coincidental.

Cover design: Nelson Kane
Interior design: PerfecType, Nashville, TN

Library of Congress Cataloging-in-Publication Data
Maul, Derek, 1956–
  10 life-charged words : real faith for men / by Derek Maul.
    p. cm.
  ISBN 978-0-8358-1116-3 — ISBN 978-0-8358-1123-1
  1. Christian men—Prayers and devotions. I. Title. II. Title: Ten life-charged words.
  BV4843.M38 2012
  248.8'42—dc23
                              2011053105

ISBN: 978-0-8358-1116-3

Printed in the United States of America

DEDICATION

To all those who own such a hunger for life
that they refuse to compromise,
to all who live according to the great "yes" of promise,
to all who love beyond the limits of reason,
to all who are willing to embrace the life-charged life,
to all those who color outside the lines.
You know who you are . . .

CONTENTS

ACKNOWLEDGMENTS

I want to kick off the acknowledgments with what amounts to an addendum to the dedication. The dedication is complete, but at the same time I need to make more than a reference to my brother, Geoff.

Geoffrey Alan Maul died March 12, 2012, after a difficult struggle with cancer. At the date of his passing we were deeply involved in a series of pivotal conversations designed to help us both understand his story. We communicated on a level that did more than exchange information; it involved spiritual healing and an almost sacramental passing of grace. We talked in depth about the "life-charged" life, and my brother embraced such life in the manner in which he lived out the balance of his days. Make no mistake, Geoff was no saint. But isn't the point of this discussion that the invitation to new and vibrant life is always before us, even in our brokenness, especially in our struggle? "In this is love, not that we loved God but that he loved us and sent his Son to be the atoning sacrifice for our sins" (1 John 4:10).

I also need to acknowledge some of the folk who continue to encourage me in my journey. Gerard, Charles, David, Grace, Jesse, Ray, Greg, members of the Men's Room, the Tims, Don, Mark. The staff at The Upper Room who are amazing and unsung:

Eli, Robin, Jeannie, Anne, Janice, Jill, Tom, Sharon, Sherry, Joanna, (intern) Andrew, Rita, Lauren, Elizabeth, Lynne . . . .

Finally my wife and best friend, Rebekah, who lives her faith out loud with both conviction and eloquence; you are my muse and the heart of my joy.

In love, and because of love—DEREK

INTRODUCTION

OK, guys, gather round. Let me have a word with you. I have a message from God. Ready?

God wants to know, "Are you in or are you out?"

"What kind of a question is that?" you say. "I go to church, I love God, and I'm even reading your book! What do you mean, 'Am I in or am I out?'"

Well, some of you do go to church; but some of you don't (and maybe for good reason). Some of us are fully involved in the faith world whereas some of us are more comfortable standing on the periphery, looking in. Regardless of where you are, I'd really like to include everyone in the conversation. But, no worries; listen in for a while and follow along for a few pages. I'd like to explain where I'm coming from.

A number of the men I talk with feel as if their spiritual life is dying on the vine or they sense that the church they attend is steadily slipping into irrelevancy. Things like this are prone to happen because too much of late twentieth-century denominational Christianity took its eye off the ball, put its feet up, and settled into a comfortable complacency (with, I might add, the full cooperation of its members). Churchgoers have become so conformed to the status quo (a modus operandi that's killing the churches they love) that any other way of doing business—even if it involves being faithful—feels like breaking faith.

What's happening is this: dynamic faith in Jesus Christ has largely given way to a new orthodoxy in the form of faith in a cultural norm (type, standard, custom, model, convention). This new orthodoxy has been described as "Christianity" for so long we've lost the ability to tell the difference.

Consequently, the religion many of us espouse and practice has become too insipid and lackluster to inspire much of a relationship with the church we say we're committed to. Instead, our relationship rarely goes beyond semiregular attendance, family membership (not unlike that gym you seldom visit), and a one-stop-shop for significant rites of passage.

Jesus Rocks

To put it more bluntly: Jesus came to rock the establishment. Now we, his followers, *are* the establishment—or we think we are (which may be worse!). Instead of defining ourselves as "followers of the Way," we have masterminded a detour that has long since ceased to challenge our refined, middle-class sensibilities.

Hope exists, however, because God is unerringly faithful, God is constantly creating and re-creating, and God has defined the future—my future and yours—in terms of promise.

Life!

When Jesus offered the possibility that his followers could experience life in all of its prolific and bounteous abundance, the Son of Man was not fooling around. Listen to the scripture from John 10:7-10. Read it aloud and take note, because this text will be coming around again in just a few chapters.

Very truly, I tell you, I am the gate for the sheep. All who came before me are thieves and bandits; but the sheep did not listen to them. I am the gate. Whoever enters by me will be saved, and will come in and go out and find pasture. The thief comes only to steal and kill and destroy. I came that they may have life, and have it abundantly.

The thief actually has been stealing and destroying. And in looking around, we realize that our churches and our Christianity too often lack the abundant life.

- Life can't be abundant if it's not, first of all, authentic.
- Real life replicates itself naturally.
- Life is irrepressible and relentless.
- Life is supposed to be part and parcel of our ongoing relationship with God.

What happens when life is not there? Well, the organism dies.

The ten words in this book come loaded with dynamic life because they represent promise and possibility for men who seriously want to build on a deliberate decision to live as disciples.

These words are not a formula so much as an invitation. They challenge us to embrace the kind of abundance Jesus was talking about when he invited those first disciples to follow him. Jesus may not want us to drop our nets or our small business or our regular lives. But Jesus is inviting us to throw out the "same old, same old" practices and understandings that lead to religious dissatisfaction and spiritual disquiet.

The fact is, God wants us to drop life-starved religion and embrace abundant life—a life lived to capacity and guided by Jesus, excellence, passion, scripture, holiness, clarity, prayer, authenticity, and community.

In short, God wants us to embrace the life of Jesus.

ONE
JESUS

For in him the whole fullness of deity dwells bodily, and you have come to fullness in him, who is the head of every ruler and authority.

COLOSSIANS 2:9-10

> *Jesus*: Jesus of Nazareth, born 4 BCE, crucified 29 CE; the inspiration for the Christian religion; the Alpha and the Omega; the Word made flesh; the supreme example of God's nature expressed through human beings. Christ, Good Shepherd, King of kings, Lamb of God, Lord, Lord of lords, Messiah, Prince of Peace, Redeemer, Savior, Son of Man.

One Sunday when my wife, Rebekah, who serves as a speaker/consultant, was visiting a struggling congregation in a distant city in another state, she was challenged regarding the message she had shared that morning.

"You sure talk about Jesus a lot," one church member said critically, exhibiting half of a frown. "Maybe it's just some Southern thing; but we're not used to hearing that much Christ-language around here."

My wife smiled when she shared this story. On the one hand, she smiled because she knew that, no, Jesus is not "some Southern thing." Jesus, and talking in "Christ-language," is a God thing. Jesus stands as God's initiative, God's complete and grace-laden answer for the brokenness of this world. On the other hand, Rebekah smiled ruefully because that comment was a clue as to why the congregation in question had been struggling for so long and why the members had felt the need to fly her in as a consultant for the weekend.

A church can go only so far on good looks, cutting-edge programs, eloquent preaching, awesome music, warm fellowship, excellent education, a happening youth group, a hearty endowment, super-cool people, and top-notch physical surroundings. All of these are important elements, but what counts most is Jesus. Jesus serves as the "life" in "life-charged," and without Jesus at the core of everything—well, the entire operation becomes little more than one more social club (and an expensive one at that).

A J.E.S.U.S. Acronym

Jesus is the ultimate life-charged word. Jesus is vital to the extreme; Jesus is exhilarating; Jesus is a name loaded with life-transforming truths. There really is, as the hymn suggests, "just something about that name."

There is undeniable power in the name of Jesus. Consequently, and while we appreciate the scope of what the Christ-life makes possible, experiencing Jesus "full on" can be overwhelming. The good news can be too much for us and we find ourselves unable to take it all in, unable to process the meaning and the truth and the challenge. And so now and then we are tempted to merely park the Savior in a safe place and keep our distance, lest we find ourselves challenged beyond reason and outside the limits of what we suppose is our capacity to process.

My recent book, *Reaching toward Easter*, concluded with a discussion about why, soon after the excitement of Easter Sunday, we find ourselves so tempted to maneuver Jesus right back into the tomb and roll the stone securely back into place. One reason is that when we take Jesus seriously, sometimes he becomes more Savior than we can deal with at once. Oh, once in a while we might be prepared to peek in and allow a partial sliver of a finger of a shaft of light to seep into our world, like daylight through a crack in the door.

So what does "Jesus" mean, and why is the name above all names such a challenge? I find it helpful to use an acronym—J.E.S.U.S.—to demonstrate how Jesus' name can spell out his message of hope and purpose in a way that we can begin to wrap our minds around. Here it is: J.E.S.U.S.—Jehovah's Extravagant Salvation and Unsearchable Sufficiency.

Jesus (according to John's Gospel) is the essence of God's nature revealed in human form. "And the Word became flesh and lived among us, and we have seen his glory, the glory as of a father's only son, full of grace and truth" (John 1:14). That's a lot to take in, but we can use the letters in "Jesus" to help us understand how God is prepared to work a life-charged intervention in each of our lives.

J Is for JEHOVAH

First, Jesus is God, and God's name is "Jehovah" (literally, YHWH in Hebrew, but the *y* comes to us as a *j* via the German transliteration; regardless, "Yeshua" [Jesus] and "YHWH" start with the same

Hebrew letter). According to the words of the Nicene Creed, God and Jesus are "of one substance." Jesus is God (YHWH), and God in Christ is alive in us.

God is the source of light and life, creator and sustainer of everything, the known and the unknown. When we think about how *Jesus* can be a life-charged word, it helps to remember that the *j* stands for every charge of energy in every facet of creation. Jesus is our invitation to fullness of life, what God intended from the very beginning. This offer of fullness is why Jesus came and explains why we can't engage such a life-charged level of life without an active relationship with Jesus.

E Is for EXTRAVAGANT

We are often tempted to tone down our spiritual lives, to not call attention to ourselves. You know, keep the lid on. *Extravagance* sounds a little too over the top, doesn't it? But the idea of "lacking restraint," while troubling to our conservative sensibilities, is precisely what Jesus offers when it comes to this redefinition of life we're considering, especially regarding our spiritual lives. "Comfortable" isn't always where we need to be if we want to move forward. As Paul put it, "if anyone is in Christ, there is a new creation: everything old has passed away; see, everything has become new!" (2 Cor. 5:17). By this measure,

- extravagant is the right word for love
- extravagant is the right word for grace
- extravagant is the right word for forgiveness
- extravagant is the right word for blessing
- extravagant is the right word for the life-charged life

The *e* in *Jesus* is about blowing the lid off.

S Is for SALVATION

The first *s* in Jesus stands for salvation. We need to understand exactly what this word means, because Christians' understanding of this concept has become skewed in the past few decades, so that salvation is often inaccurately represented. Yes, Jesus came to save us, but Jesus came to save us *for* something as much as *from* something. Salvation is not so much about "pie in the sky when we die" as it is about life that means something today.

The biblical narrative most persistently and consistently depicts salvation as "participating in the work of God." In other words, the salvation Jesus offers is an invitation to live as if God, in Jesus, truly has offered each of us the opportunity to participate in this extravagant, life-charged life. When we know Jesus, we are saved into the dynamic life and purpose of the extravagant love of God.

U Is for UNSEARCHABLE

Much about Jesus remains a deep mystery—unsearchable, inscrutable, hidden. In spite of this, many Christians want to understand the mystery of Jesus through the use of reason, stereotyping, reasonability, argument, explanation, preference, and even predictability. These attempts serve as another symptom of how we want to craft a God we can manage. When we remold or remodel Jesus into a mirror image of ourselves, so that the Lord morphs from the incarnation of the living God into someone who shares our narrow and idiosyncratic political opinions, then we're no longer talking about the same Jesus—not the life-charged Jesus, not the Jesus who threatens to make over my life or the Jesus who promises to transform yours, not the Jesus described in scripture.

O the depth of the riches and wisdom and knowledge of God! How unsearchable are his judgments and how inscrutable his ways! (Rom. 11:33).

In whom are hidden all the treasures of wisdom and knowledge (Col. 2:3).

Can you find out the deep things of God? Can you find out the limit of the Almighty? (Job 11:7).

S Is for SUFFICIENCY

Our culture's constant stress on self-sufficiency can create a gulf between our approach to life and the Christian vision of the way of the disciple. Who among us hasn't felt the pressure to "do it myself"? However, when we're thinking about the life-charged life, then strict self-sufficiency becomes a posture that works against life. Jesus is sufficient, and one challenge we face as men is the difficulty we have with trust.

But [Jesus] said to me, "My grace is sufficient for you, for power is made perfect in weakness." So, I will boast all the more gladly of my weaknesses, so that the power of Christ may dwell in me (2 Cor. 12:9).

Jesus Lifts Us Up

We've already discussed the fact that Jesus can be too much to handle. Jesus can be a challenge if we take him seriously, and so we often find ways to avoid him altogether. Part of this effort may stem from a concern that we not come across as the kind of believers who always seem to point out the negative. We don't talk about

Jesus because, you know, we don't want people to mistake us for "those kind of people."

But keeping Jesus under wraps is the wrong approach if we honestly are concerned that people are getting the wrong message. Instead of disassociating from Jesus, we need to distance ourselves from the many lies being perpetuated in Christ's name. Such as:

- the lie that Jesus has a favored political party
- the lie that God's blessings always translate into financial gain
- the lie that "God hates _____ (fill in your personal prejudice here)
- the lie that "God helps those who help themselves" and that we have no social obligation to care for the poor

And so it makes sense to learn to know Jesus more intimately. Then, based on that newfound knowledge, we'll be well equipped to communicate the truth about Jesus rather than let the extremists have the stage.

In other words, if all we do is identify ourselves in terms of the negative, then we're the opposite of life-charged. Instead, we're antilife: "Well, we're not like this," or "We're not like them," or "We're most certainly not like that." Most of us know church people who not only appear to be against everything but also don't mind telling us about it. But Jesus calls us to embrace everything that we can be in Christ, to celebrate the doors that are now open, and to step into the many possibilities that are now ours. So forget the can'ts, the shan'ts, the don'ts, and the won'ts; our invitation is to live "into" Jesus. The Lord put it this way to the Pharisees; his emphasis is on the word *shall*.

> When the Pharisees heard that he had silenced the Sadducees, they gathered together, and one of them, a lawyer, asked him

a question to test him. "Teacher, which commandment in the law is the greatest?" He said to him, "You shall love the Lord your God with all your heart, and with all your soul, and with all your mind. This is the greatest and first commandment. And a second is like it: You shall love your neighbor as yourself. On these two commandments hang all the law and the prophets." (Matt. 22:34-40).

We create a sad witness when we present the public face of our faith in the negative, but that doesn't mean those of us seeking to live a life-charged faith should fall into the "not like them" trap too.

- you are not "those people"
- I am not "those people"
- instead, we are called to be "Jesus people"!

So let's demonstrate to the world that Jesus is the Lord of the positive, not the champion of the "thou shalt nots"! The thrust of new life in Jesus is affirmative, upbeat, positive, and encouraging. "I can do all things through [Christ] who strengthens me" (Phil. 4:13).

The Acts of the Apostles gives an epic account of Jesus' earliest followers, who did not define themselves in the negative as compared to the world around them. Instead, they simply shared the good news of salvation and participated in what God was doing in this world. And guess what? Their message also became popular among the common people in Jerusalem.

Day by day, as they spent much time together in the temple, they broke bread at home and ate their food with glad and generous hearts, praising God and having the goodwill of all the people. And day by day the Lord added to their number those who were being saved (Acts 2:46-47).

Peter and John didn't stand on the street corner and proclaim that the people were going to hell. Instead they told them about "What we have seen and heard" (Acts 4:20).

Likewise, Paul didn't tell the people in Athens that their gods were "of the devil," or that they were on the fast track to you know where. Instead, Paul invited them to come to know the same Jesus who had transformed his life.

> Then Paul stood in front of the Areopagus and said, "Athenians, I see how extremely religious you are in every way. For as I went through the city and looked carefully at the objects of your worship, I found among them an altar with the inscription, 'To an unknown god.' What therefore you worship as unknown, this I proclaim to you" (Acts 17:22-23).

When we allow Jesus to shine through us, people see the gospel of light and life, not the edict of doom and gloom. If we lose the Jesus part of the equation, then we have lost the life-charged part of our faith. If other things take priority—no matter how important they may be—then we are seriously off balance in what we do.

Jesus Is the Engine That Drives Everything

OK, here's a question: If you're part of a Christian congregation, what role do you play in the church? What's your involvement or responsibility?

- Do you serve as an elder or on the church board?
- Are you a deacon, a small group leader, or a Sunday school teacher?
- Do you work with facilities or in finance?

- Do you chair a ministry team, play the piano, sing in the choir, or lock up the building after church?

Whatever our involvement in the church may be, our natural tendency is to focus on that priority, that activity, or that particular agenda. We often do this at the expense of remembering that Jesus is the only priority that truly matters.

We can easily imagine the conversation; in fact we may have heard similar arguments on more than one occasion out in the parking lot after worship: Church should be about quality music—that's what's going to bring people in the door. Or, we need to make sure our Sunday school teachers are top-notch and then you'll see that the children will come in droves. Or, what people need is to hear sound doctrine, like we did back when I was a young person. Or, what's most important is the church grounds. First impressions mean everything if we want more than a drive-by from potential visitors. Or, we need the pastor to speak out from the pulpit and to take a stand on political issues so people will know how to take a Christian position. Or, we have to be feeding the homeless and caring for those on the edge of losing everything. Mission and outreach are going to make this church strong!

And so it goes—mission, education, finances, evangelism, justice, doctrine, youth, children's ministry. All of these are very important aspects of the Church's mission. But the answer, the life-charged word that should always be first and foremost on our hearts and minds whatever we're focusing on in the church or at home, is Jesus!

Let the same mind be in you that was in Christ Jesus, who, though he was in the form of God, did not regard equality with God as something to be exploited, but emptied himself, taking the form of a slave, being born in human likeness.

And being found in human form, he humbled himself and became obedient to the point of death—even death on a cross. Therefore God also highly exalted him and gave him the name that is above every name, so that at the name of Jesus every knee should bend, in heaven and on earth and under the earth, and every tongue should confess that Jesus Christ is Lord, to the glory of God the Father (Phil. 2:5-11).

We Want to Be Strong

Part and parcel of our "man vibe" is the desire to be thought of as strong. I'm sure many of us have tried to move heavy boxes, a piano, or furniture that we had no business even thinking about lifting. We accept tasks beyond our comfort zone exactly because we know it will take everything we have and then some. We grit our teeth and try because we honestly do believe that our manhood depends on our performance, our verve, our courage, our willingness to take it on—whatever "it" may be.

Now listen up (and I'm going to surprise some of you with this statement)—Jesus understands. Not only that, but Jesus respects the core idea, that inner drive motivating us that often ends up looking like false bravado.

Jesus understands men! The Lord is all about the bottom line, the "all or nothing," the dig-deep-in-your-gut-and-show-them-what-you've-got attitude that so often drives us. Jesus understands.

But for Jesus, digging deep means something different than we think (which always seemed the case with Jesus). For Jesus, digging deep begins spiritually. Starting from the perspective of faith is a principle God has advocated consistently. "Not by might, nor by power, but by my spirit, says the LORD of hosts" (Zech. 4:6). Not by might or by power but by the Spirit of God.

When we live our lives from such a faithful grounding, the bottom line that motivates us becomes a Jesus event. Unlike regular events, Jesus events are charged with life and purpose and the very energy that birthed light and life into the substance of this world.

Jesus Wants In on the Conversation

Another way of saying this is that Jesus wants to be part of the conversation of our day-to-day lives. There's nearly no way to start the ball rolling other than cold turkey; we either make the choice to include the Lord in the daily routine or we don't. The life-charged Jesus, salt and light, an empowering and life-giving presence, mentor and guide.

So here's an idea that might help. Pull out your best felt-tip marker, and write a *J*, an *E*, an *S*, a *U*, and an *S* on five coins. Place them in your left pocket. Then, during each day, whenever you're tempted to jangle your change, pull out a coin, consider the meaning of the letter you've extracted, and then place the coin in your right-hand pocket.

Did you pull out the *E*? Then spend a minimum of one minute thinking about the extravagance of grace, of love, and of Jesus' faithfulness. Then thank God for the gift.

Maybe the next letter is an *S*, and you go through the same process regarding what it means to participate in the ongoing work of God via salvation or the amazing sufficiency of Jesus.

Each day, five coins.

After several weeks you can up the ante by finding creative ways to introduce the concept from each coin into conversation with a friend, your spouse, or a colleague at work. One coin per day; five over the course of a week.

When the Christ-life begins to inhabit our conscious, our subconscious, and even our reflexive thought patterns, Jesus will necessarily make an impact on every aspect of our being. "And remember," the great teacher promised, "I am with you always, to the end of the age" (Matt. 28:20).

Now that's a promise that will add a charge to your life!

The Bottom Line

- Without Jesus, church is nothing but another version of a nice social club.
- Jesus understands men.
- Don't simply report back to God later; invite Jesus along.
- Rather than slow us down, Jesus adds life to the details of life.
- Where religion seeks to regulate, Jesus promises to animate.
- J.E.S.U.S. = Jehovah's Extravagant Salvation and Unsearchable Sufficiency.
- Next time you read the New Testament, notice how the presence of Jesus always results in new and vibrant life.

Let's Talk about It

Use these questions for personal reflection, in reading this book with a couple of friends, or for discussion as a study group in your faith community.

1. Who is Jesus to you? Think of five words that describe who Jesus is in your life. Write them down and (if participating in a small group) share them around the circle.
2. Think of five words that describe who you would like Jesus to be in your life. Again, write the words down and share them.

3. What drives the ministry of your faith community? Is it Jesus or do other areas (politics, finances, education, tradition) take precedence?

4. The J.E.S.U.S. acronym may be a useful device for keeping the life-charged nature of Jesus in our awareness. You may think of different attributes to hang on the letters (such as, "e" is for "example," Christ is my "example"; or "encourager"). Suggest some, share what they mean to you, and how, specifically, these are life-charged attributes.

5. A friend once suggested that Jesus was a "force multiplier" in his life. Identify a situation where Jesus could have that effect on your life in the coming days.

PRAYER: Great God of Creation, we humbly admit that we tend to pigeonhole you at every turn and that the light, life, and creative motivation of Jesus is always far more than we can hope or imagine in our lives. Please take our reading, our discussion, and our living and infuse all that we are with your life and your amazing love. We want to understand you more, but we are also conscious of your transcendence. We are thankful for the ways that Jesus helps us to close the gap between your greatness and our need. Amen.

EXCELLENCE

TWO

The steward called the bridegroom and said to him, "Everyone serves the good wine first, and then the inferior wine after the guests have become drunk. But you have kept the good wine until now." Jesus did this, the first of his signs, in Cana of Galilee, and revealed his glory; and his disciples believed in him.

JOHN 2:9-11

Excellence: Surpassing accomplishment, eminently good, outstanding, distinguishable by superiority.

Gourmet: Connoisseur; interested in flavor and all that is good; one who appreciates the best.

"Be excellent to each other and party on dudes." *Bill & Ted's Excellent Adventure*

*E*xcellent may not accurately describe all Christians in all circumstances, but the idea is spot on when it comes to describing the intention of the gospel message with regard to how we are called to handle daily living.

> Finally, beloved, whatever is true, whatever is honorable, whatever is just, whatever is pure, whatever is pleasing, whatever is commendable, if there is any excellence and if there is anything worthy of praise, think about these things (Phil. 4:8).

A Life-charged Word to Live By

Excellence is a life-charged word that calls to the best in us. What this world needs is an epidemic of "most excellent" followers of Jesus, those who are brilliant, outstanding, and first-rate in Christ.

More than being excellent in their relationships to one another, Christian men are called to model excellence in all things. What each of us needs, both as individuals and in our relationships, is a commitment to the very best—distinction, quality, and merit—in every aspect of the way that we live.

Words such as *mediocrity, indolence, apathy,* and *disinterest* have no place in the spirit-animated life. God created each of us with unique qualities and equipped us to become the very best we possibly can:

- as men
- as spiritual people
- as communities of faith
- as partners
- as employers and employees
- as dads
- as citizens of this world

- as stewards of our bodies
- as friends
- and as lovers

We disrespect the intention of creation if we live our lives in any other way.

A Gospel of Excellence for Most Excellent Dudes

In the Gospel of John, the writer weaves a captivating narrative around seven distinct miracles.

- Jesus turned water into really good wine (John 2:1-11). "You have kept the good wine until now."
- Jesus restored a child with a dangerous fever (John 4:46-54). "Now this was the second sign."
- Jesus healed a paralyzed man at the pool by the Sheep Gate (John 5:1-14). "Do you want to be made well?"
- Jesus fed five thousand hungry people (John 6:1-14). "They were satisfied."
- Jesus calmed a tumultuous storm on the Sea of Galilee (John 6:16-21). "It is I; do not be afraid."
- Jesus healed a blind man (John 9:1-7). "As long as I am in the world, I am the light of the world."
- Jesus raised Lazarus from death (John 11:1-44). "I am the resurrection and the life."

Jesus, of course, was a walking miracle. Nothing about the travelling teacher was the least bit ordinary or predictable or run-of-the-mill—from the way he dealt with people to the amazing words that he spoke. Every moment spent in the presence of Jesus had to have been charged with life and expectation.

John's story bristles with animation and vitality from start to finish; it is rich, deeply nuanced, and lit up with transformational language. The text is radiant in terms of its spiritual aura. Yet John limited the number of miracles or "signs" that he included in the narrative to merely seven, although he could have included many more (see John 21:25), a detail that surprises many people. John's focus was not on the miraculous nature of Jesus' ministry.

The realization that John's narrative isn't driven by other-worldliness tells us a lot. The life-charged life isn't about the miraculous so much as it is about a sense of fullness, of transcendent life, and of unremitting quality.

John's telling of the Jesus story testifies to the value of excellence and the power of the extraordinary to effect transformational change.

That's How Jesus Rolled

The first miracle in John's Gospel describes the wedding festival in Cana, when Jesus changed ordinary water into wine. Not just any wine, but wine that drew the attention of the chief steward because it was "most excellent."

So right off the bat, John makes a quiet, subtle, actions-speak-louder-than-words statement that whenever anything happens in the immediate vicinity of Jesus, that event will be top-notch, first-rate, and as good as it gets. It doesn't matter what the occasion involves, whether a simple meal, preaching, conversation, stories around the campfire, Bible study, casual discourse, or even the beverage selection at a wedding bash. What mattered was quality. If Jesus was involved, then the occasion would be marked by excellence, bottom line. The best of the best of the very, very best.

When the servants at the wedding followed directions (and following Jesus' directions is always a good rule of thumb whenever we find ourselves in this ongoing conversation about the life-charged life), I find it interesting that they filled the water pitchers "to the brim." This statement marks the relationship between excellence and another one of our life-charged words, *capacity*. For there is nothing halfway about Jesus' quality of excellence. No half measures, no holding back. The Christ-life fills us to overflowing, and we are satisfied. No need to get drunk, no need to binge, no need to settle for second best.

The Gourmet Life

One of the best Christmas gifts I've ever given serves as a helpful commentary when it comes to the life-charged life. On Christmas of 2009 I presented my wife with three new cookbooks and a card with this message: "Rebekah, this is a gift that will last the year long. Each week during 2010 I want you to pick out one recipe you've always wanted to try. Show me the page, and I'll prepare the recipe exactly as written. These three new cookbooks have some great ideas, but you can find anything you'd like me to cook in any cookbook you want. I love you, always.—DEREK"

I should mention that ever since our children were in elementary school I've been the primary cook in our household. Not by plan but basically because it worked out that way, given my wife's and my schedules. And (if I say so myself) I've always done a fairly decent job in the kitchen. But since I've never been afraid to tinker with my recipes, as a result, over the years a lot of my core menu items lost their distinctiveness and started to blur together. A kind of generic-Derek style emerged.

The gift to my wife that year turned into a great opportunity for me to learn some new cooking techniques. As a result, I broke out of the generic-Derek style and became a stickler for following directions. I've been "doing it right" ever since.

So what did it take for me to break out of the ordinary with regard to my habits in the kitchen?

1. Learn a new set of fundamentals in order to prepare the specific sauces and styles that are called for.
2. Research and practice various and often unfamiliar techniques.
3. Take the time to use the exact herbs and spices rather than limiting myself to the ones I like.
4. Shop around to find unusual ingredients and then learn what to do with them.

For example, if your favorite dish in the world is lasagna, going from popping something prepackaged into the oven to actually preparing the recipe from scratch is guaranteed to take a lot of work and to be a challenge. Excellence requires reading the cookbook, paying close attention to the details, and following the instructions.

How about crushing and chopping fresh sweet basil leaves rather than using the fossilized specimens from your spice rack? Making your own marinara sauce? Using four different cheeses? Asking questions at the grocery store?

I quickly learned that using fresh ingredients does make a huge difference; that using an exact amount of oregano and a precisely measured quantity of thyme is far better than the dash of "mixed Italian spices"; that the correct balance of mozzarella cheese, ricotta cheese, cottage cheese, and Parmesan cheese does yield amazing results; and that sautéing the mushrooms first will pay dividends when the dish is served later.

The End of Half-measures

The shift in quality that I experienced in my cooking serves as a fair description of what happens to a man's spiritual life when his walk with God moves from so-so to life-charged. As a result, the relationship with the Creator is no longer humdrum but characterized by light and life, fragrance and flavor.

In the long run, faith, like cooking, occasionally becomes familiar and comfortable (perhaps too comfortable). Maybe we've always been pretty good at doing this Christian thing, and maybe God has been a part of our daily life for decades. But if we are honest, we have to admit that, just like the food, the results can often be mediocre and boring. We can be guilty of "on-the-fly" faith, of using generic spiritual ingredients, of being happy to have enough skill to make our spiritual life work but never coming close to being a threat in terms of greatness.

The sad truth for too many of us, too much of the time, when it comes to the bottom line about spiritual life, is that we fall into this category: "Never came close to being a threat in terms of greatness."

But the good news is that we can learn to become open to authentic growth. We can learn to build our relationship with God on fresh experiences rather than borrowed, prepackaged, flash-frozen, or canned ingredients. We can learn that being a follower of the Way involves much more than okay, good enough, adequate, or this'll do. We can learn this *because the promise of Jesus is the ending of half-measures.*

Each of us can make this decision by adopting this statement as our daily mantra: "Today I will listen to the urging of the Spirit rather than fall back on the comfortable habits of the past." Then the best ingredients can come together and work in concert in response to this simple, ongoing decision to follow Jesus.

Bon appétit.

Excellence Leads to Balance

The Centers for Disease Control now classifies obesity as an epidemic in North America. Everything from bariatric surgery to strict dieting and regular exercise is being touted as a potential solution. Doctors estimate that 40 percent of America's health care expenditures could be eliminated if people were able to keep their body mass index in the normal range.

One creative approach to this problem is excellence in cooking—specifically, educating ourselves in the preparation and consumption of higher quality food. This educating involves not only eating leaner and healthier foods but also paying attention to flavor; that is, to excellence. Simply eating foods that are more flavorful and naturally satisfying addresses a fundamental principle on the continuum of overconsumption.

We eat too much for the same reasons we pursue anything to excess. We're not satisfied, so we consume more and more. That is the fundamental lack that leads to overconsumption. When the food we're eating—or the lifestyle we've chosen or the priorities we're pursuing or the addiction we're being controlled by—is inherently unable to satisfy us, then we become caught in a vicious cycle of escalating consumption without satisfaction. This loop can be a black hole of perpetual disappointment that leads to desire for more and more of what remains unsatisfying and always will.

However (sticking with the cooking analogy), great food that is both nutritious and bursting with amazing flavor is always satisfying. We don't need to gorge ourselves with garbage when we're already fulfilled and content.

The Big Question (and Why We're So Confused)

Why do so many of us settle for freeze-dried, prepackaged, microwavable, plastic-wrapped lives? God created us to enjoy the very best. Excellence serves as its own reward.

Jesus can help here. Jesus pointed out the danger of assigning the attribute of *excellence* to the wrong things:

> Do not store up for yourselves treasures on earth, where moth and rust consume and where thieves break in and steal; but store up for yourselves treasures in heaven, where neither moth nor rust consumes and where thieves do not break in and steal (Matt. 6:19-20).

Similarly, the writer of the book of Ecclesiastes noted the same fundamental disconnect. "I saw all the deeds that are done under the sun; and see, all is vanity and a chasing after wind. What is crooked cannot be made straight, and what is lacking cannot be counted" (1:14-15).

No longer listening to the false voices that elbow their way into our consciousness and deceive us is critically important. Otherwise, we become hoodwinked into the pursuit of values and priorities that are guaranteed to trap hearts and minds in a cycle of dependence and dissatisfaction. Alternatively, we could pay attention, as Abraham Lincoln said so poetically in his first inaugural address, to "the better angels of our nature."

So What?

The implementation of excellence as a life-charged value is, more often than not, basically a matter of purposeful application. Let's consider some provocative questions:

- Do you see yourself, at the core of who you are as a child of God, as a joint heir with Christ (Rom. 8:17), someone who has "been raised with Christ" (Col. 3:1)? Or do you believe that excellence is only the province of a few special people?
- When you give, do you bring your very best? Or do you merely trundle out your leftovers?
- You can be engaging and charming at work, but do you bring your finest behavior to the table when you sit down at a meal with your wife or your family?
- You have been gifted with creativity and imagination, but how much of that do you use on behalf of the men's ministry at church?
- The Bible points out that our physical bodies are the temple of the Holy Spirit (1 Cor. 6:19). Does the way you stay in shape (or the way you fail to) glorify God at all? What does your physical body honor?
- How do you manage your finances? Are you a faithful steward of your resources?
- How about time? Do you use your time wisely?
- Do you nourish your mind through learning, culture, and stimulating conversation or do you settle for cheap and tawdry entertainment that fails to satisfy yet sucks you in? Remember:

Finally, beloved, whatever is true, whatever is honorable, whatever is just, whatever is pure, whatever is pleasing, whatever is commendable, if there is any excellence and if there is anything worthy of praise, think about these things (Phil. 4:8).

Infusion of Life

Excellence is not about one upping others or a competition that requires someone else to fail in order for us to win. Excellence is about honing and using the particular gifts we were equipped with when we were shaped and fashioned as people made in the image of the Creator.

Tapping into that truth requires us to embrace the Spirit that Jesus employed to animate everything that he said or did. Everyone around Jesus was infused with life because excellence defined the way the great teacher interacted with the world.

Final Illustration

I have made reference to my brother, Geoff, more than once in this book. He is, at the time of this writing, preoccupied with what may turn out to be a life-and-death struggle with cancer. His is the kind of tragedy that most of us seem to run into at one time or another. In a recent conversation with me, Geoff took issue with one particular cliché that's been making the rounds. Someone had advised him, "Live each day as if it were your last."

"They meant well," Geoff said, "but I worked in hospitals as a respiratory therapist for many years, and most people aren't doing so well on their last day. I'm more inclined to go with the other end of the equation, 'Live each day as if it were your first!'"

I like that. I like the inspiration of freshness, newborn enthusiasm, unlimited promise, and the wide-open spirit that's aching to learn and breathe and take in everything that life has to offer. God's kind of excellence resides in such a life-charged commitment to the gift that is—always—today.

The Bottom Line

- We easily slip into mediocrity.
- Excellence is not only a good idea but also a spiritual value.
- Excellence in all that you do can be a strong witness in spreading the gospel message.
- Live each day as if it were your first.
- Excellence is the best solution to the malady of "too much."
- Rekindle the "gift of God that is within you" on a regular basis. Paul reminds Timothy that excellence is "the gift of God that is within you," and he points out that the gift could use routine rekindling.

For this reason I remind you to rekindle the gift of God that is within you through the laying on of my hands; for God did not give us a spirit of cowardice, but rather a spirit of power and of love and of self-discipline (2 Tim. 1:6-7).

Let's Talk about It

Use these questions for personal reflection, in reading this book with a couple of friends, or for discussion as a study group in your faith community.

1. What idea (or ideas) from the Bible does the phrase "Be excellent to one another" bring to mind?

2. Imagine launching a new day in the context of embracing excellence as your modus operandi. Imagine getting out of bed; what's the first thing you would change from your typical routine?

3. If you applied the principle of excellence to your most important relationships, what kind of changes might be forthcoming?

4. In embracing the truth that we were fashioned in the image of the Creator, pinpoint three specific things you could do to honor excellence in body and mind.

5. How do you believe excellence might add a life-charged element to your life as a man? as a person of faith? as a husband? as a professional? as a church member? as a friend?

6. Several scriptures were cited in this chapter. Which text spoke to you most profoundly? Explain how.

PRAYER: Great God who created the heavens and the earth and then remarked how good it was, thank you for showing us the way to excellence through the example of the life of Jesus. Be with us as we do our best to live in the truth of your most excellent purposes for our lives. Amen.

THREE
PASSION

But this one thing I do: forgetting what lies behind and straining forward to what lies ahead, I press on toward the goal for the prize of the heavenly call of God in Christ Jesus.

PHILIPPIANS 3:13-14

Passion: Intense conviction; boundless enthusiasm; compelling emotion.

It was an unseasonably hot spring afternoon at the annual Strawberry Festival in Plant City, Florida. The midway was crowded. The sticky, sweet atmosphere featured the aroma of strawberry shortcake, cotton candy, hot dogs, fresh pretzels, and the latest version of "let's put one of these on a stick and deep-fry it in fat to see what it tastes like!"

Rebekah and I were there to see our eighth-grade son play clarinet in his middle-school marching band. We were sitting in the stands at the end of the two-mile parade route. The kids were tired and the temperature was pushing ninety degrees.

Several school bands marched by in various states of disarray and distress. Some of the kids were carrying their instruments instead of playing them; the directors were walking alongside the bands without directing, jackets slung over their shoulders, ties discarded, music abandoned, and their bands no longer in formation.

When our son's band came into view, we expected more of the same. Imagine our surprise when, with their heads held high and belting out clear notes from their instruments, our son and his friends marched into the stadium at full pace, playing "When the Saints Go Marching In" as if the song had been written explicitly about them.

Mr. Lewis, their director, in stark contrast to the other teachers, still wore his coat and tie, with every button in place. He faced his band, walking backward, arms stretched out above his head and conducting vigorously.

Passion is a powerful concept. That day, Mr. Lewis and the Burns Middle School Band demonstrated that they had it in spades.

We Want It; We Don't Want It

Passion is one of those concepts that we can be a little afraid of when it comes to living as twenty-first century Christian men. After all, we measure one another by ideals such as self-control, detachment, and reserve. So when we see passion in action, we find ourselves pulling back. We can't argue that it's not exactly what we need, but passion makes us nervous. We may be thirsty for the enthusiasm, but we want to experience it on our own terms. We're not ready to give ourselves to anything we can't quite control.

Let's Not Get Carried Away

We seem to accept passion in marching bands, football players, political speech makers, and artists on the stage or in movies. We actually admire it. But we tend to shy away from "that kind of thing" when it comes to personal or corporate faith.

As men, in particular, we're often uncomfortable about demonstrating too much enthusiasm in matters of devotion. We may cite reasons such as decorum, balance, embarrassment, or "not wanting to get carried away." But what's closer to the truth is that in truth we're still wrestling with our allegiance to God, and we don't know if we want to do much more than paddle around the edges of commitment. We find it nearly impossible to be passionate about something when we're still fundamentally unwilling to go all in.

Passion may be one of those words that's becoming culturally cliché; but when it comes to actual modus operandi, it seems the idea seldom shows up. The phrase "I'm passionate about _____" (fill in the blank) has been reduced to a throwaway platitude, stuffed too many times in job resumés, personal biographies, commercials, and political campaigns.

- "No one will be more passionate about representing you than candidate so-and-so."
- "I am passionate about people. If you hire me you can count on someone who is passionate about my work."
- "I'm thirty-six years old, easy to get along with, and passionate. I'm passionate about world hunger, the Rolling Stones, the 'American Idol' competition, and all God's furry creatures."

We use the same word to describe not only the way we feel about the cruel death of millions of starving people but also a popular television show. *Passion* is definitely a word at risk of the ravages of overuse. Using any concept so much and to such little effect can make it irrelevant or functionally worthless.

Passion from the Word of Life

Listen to these words from one of John's letters to some first-century Christians:

> We declare to you what was from the beginning, what we have heard, what we have seen with our eyes, what we have looked at and touched with our hands, concerning the word of life—this life was revealed, and we have seen it and testify to it, and declare to you the eternal life that was with the Father and was revealed to us—we declare to you what we have seen and heard so that you also may have fellowship with us; and truly our fellowship is with the Father and with his Son Jesus Christ. We are writing these things so that our joy may be complete (1 John 1:1-4).

Now there's a passion that delivers! Ardor, compelling feeling, powerful emotion, intense conviction—life-charged faith. John was communicating about something he knew, firsthand, and he wanted to share the joy of it with his friends.

For John, a living and vital relationship with God was the top priority when it came to sharing the good news with anyone else. I don't know about you, but every time I see a faith-based organization struggling, I want to ask some questions about the story that its leaders and members are living out in their own lives. Because, ultimately, this journey into a life-charged experience with God begins with our willingness to share something real.

That's why the best way to grow a church is to make passionate disciples. Disciples let the Christ-life spill over naturally into every aspect of day-to-day life.

Compelling Newspaper Stories

Over the past few years I've written a number of stories for newspapers and magazines—so many that I've lost count. Most of them focus on the lives of interesting people and the impact these folks have made on the community. So I've had conversations with a wide variety of men and women who are involved with activities and professions that run the gamut from preachers, musicians, CEO's, doctors, lawyers, fitness gurus, teachers, salespeople, artists, writers, chefs, politicians, and many more. These individuals work in construction, education, law, personal development, small business, farming, the church, healthcare—you name it.

But one common thread runs through practically every story: passion. I've discovered that without passion (and this does happen once in a while) there's no reason for me to run the story.

When I sit down and chat with people for an hour or more, I find it hard to avoid eventually tapping into their passion, no matter how resilient they think they can be (and people do tend to put up walls). At that point the interview becomes, quite literally, a whole new story. Invariably I have to disregard everything we had talked about up to that moment and start the story anew.

People who are fired up about what they do always make great stories. Wouldn't it be awesome (and I employ that much-overused word with deliberate care) if people tapped us on the shoulder and asked to hear more about our faith because our passion for God was so obvious and authentic?

Too True

I like to share the following story about a man who visited a church for the first time. The account is impossible to verify and may not be historical, but the absence of a footnote makes it a better illustration (in my opinion), because it can be tailored to fit any particular circumstance, church, or denomination.

The man—let's call him Ernie—walked up the steps and through the front door of an established main street church. He was handed a bulletin by an usher (who failed to greet him). Ernie made his own way down the aisle and found a seat in an unoccupied pew, which wasn't too hard considering the church was less than one quarter full.

Things went along well enough during the call to worship, the singing of the first hymn, and on through the anthem, the Bible reading, and the collection of tithes and offerings. But then, five minutes into the sermon, Ernie suddenly raised both his hands and called out a loud "Amen!" in response to one of the preacher's points.

The preacher stopped, aghast; the people shuffled in their seats; a huge silence descended; and every eye in the sanctuary turned on the visitor.

After a moment the preacher continued with his message. But again, a minute or so later, Ernie jumped to his feet, hollered, "Praise the Lord! You preach it, brother!" and sat down again.

This time a much longer silence ensued, followed by a few well-placed, meaningful coughs. Murmurs of dissent could be heard coming from the choir. The preacher, unsure of how to proceed and beet red from embarrassment, glared in the general direction of the man and then returned to his text.

The next time—and the next time came very soon—the enthusiastic visitor jumped to his feet, clapped his hands in excitement, and yelled, "Yes, Lord. Thank you Jesus. Hallelujah! Now you're preaching!"

An usher was promptly dispatched to handle the disruptive guest.

"Is everything all right, sir?" the usher whispered politely.

"Why yes. Why do you ask?" Ernie replied.

"We couldn't help noticing that you've been jumping up from your seat and calling out. You sounded distressed. Are you quite sure everything is all right?"

"Oh, I'm fine, really I am," Ernie responded. "I can't help myself; I've got the Spirit, you know!"

"Sir," the usher replied quickly, with as much dignity as he could muster, "I can assure you that you didn't get it here."

People always laugh when I share this story. I think we laugh because it strikes uncomfortably close to the truth. We laugh because most of us can envision exactly the same reaction at our own churches and can hear our ushers (bless their hearts) saying exactly the same thing. And sadly, we can imagine ourselves reacting precisely as that church reacted as well.

Passion Can Carry Us Through

"But if you are able to do anything, have pity on us and help us," [the father of the boy cried out]. Jesus said to him, "If you are able!—All things can be done for the one who believes" (Mark 9:22-23).

In this story from Mark's Gospel, Jesus appears genuinely surprised at the hold unbelief has on the people he has come to reach. He is astounded that the father of the sick boy uses the word *if* in relation to what is possible for God.

Jesus' response illustrates the strong relationship between belief and passion. We watch preschool children throw themselves into play and learning and creativity, as if enthusiasm and zeal are a natural response to this life. Then, as we age over the years, we slowly lose that initial enthusiasm, and life becomes tainted with caution and disbelief.

In a recent TED lecture (TED—Technology, Entertainment and Design—is a nonprofit devoted to "Ideas Worth Spreading"), British researcher Sir Ken Robinson commented that, while the majority of children are born with a remarkable passion for creativity, by the time they reach eighteen the natural faculty is all but gone. The only variable that can account for such a devastating loss, Robinson suggested, is thirteen years of formal education that painstakingly trains students "out of their creativity." We fail to get the best out of our students, he says, because we focus solely on preparing them to be good workers while ignoring energy and curiosity.

Many of us know new Christians who are amazed at the lack of zeal displayed by their new friends at church. Then they fall into the routine, the passionless pattern of "this is the way things work around here." I wonder how long it will be before we educate the enthusiasm right out of them? We inadvertently send the message, "I understand that everything's fresh and new for you now, but if you keep coming back to the men's meeting, we'll make sure you're as dispassionate and unimaginative as the rest of us."

Lessons from the Family Dog

Sometimes the family dog can serve as a better teacher than more traditional sources. Those of you with dogs know the routine; those without dogs, just follow along.

It starts the moment you get out of bed and walk across the floor. You can hear Fido's tail thumping on the bedroom floor: "Oh boy! Daddy's up! If I'm lucky he'll go out into the kitchen!"

Eventually of course, you do. And Fido is right there, waiting by the sink, lying on his side on the tile floor, pretending to sleep. But you can see his eyes follow you all the way to the refrigerator. He can't help but thump the floor with his tail once again.

So you down a glass of orange juice and start the coffeepot. Fido knows what's coming and can barely contain his excitement: "Daddy's going to go for my leash, I just know it. Walk time. Oh boy, oh boy, oh boy!"

And off you go. Walk on the grass? "Oh boy!" Cross the road? "Oh boy, oh boy!!" Turn down this street or that one? "Oh boy, oh boy, oh boy!!!"

Eventually you make it back home and Fido is still as excited. He can't wait to go back into the house, can't wait to check the water bowl, can't wait to eat breakfast, can't wait to go with you to take mama her coffee. "This is great! This is the best! This is the most wonderful morning I've had since—well—since yesterday morning!"

But Fido's reaction is deeper than simply "Oh boy!" There's a huge dose of gratitude along with the passionate enthusiasm. Fido looks at you as if to say, "Thank-you. Thank you so much for this life. I love you, I love you, I love you. There's a reason my tail won't stop wagging, you know."

I think the psalmist approached God with that kind of enthusiasm when he sang.

> Make a joyful noise to the LORD, all the earth.
>   Worship the LORD with gladness;
>   come into his presence with singing.
> Know that the LORD is God.

It is he that made us, and we are his;
    we are his people, and the sheep of his pasture.
Enter his gates with thanksgiving,
    and his courts with praise.
    Give thanks to him, bless his name.
For the LORD is good;
    his steadfast love endures forever,
    and his faithfulness to all generations.

Psalm 100

AMEN! (Oh boy, oh boy!)

The Root of Passion

Belief is the root of passion. Or, to turn the statement around: generating passion for anything is impossible unless we are first and foremost sold-out believers.

Belief is the answer if we're serious about ramping up the level of passion in our experience of personal faith. And belief, more than most of us seem to understand, is something we must actively choose. If we wait for belief to drop on us from above as a kind of fait accompli, then we're missing the whole point, and life-charged passion will never define who we are as Christian men.

Frank had been talking with his friends in the men's group about acting with love and respect at home and about taking deliberate steps each day to follow through with loving acts and love-loaded statements.

"But guys," he said. "Often I don't feel loving at all. Wouldn't it be hypocritical to say, 'I love you' if I didn't feel it, to embrace my wife if I don't want to, to bring flowers when I'm feeling resentful, or to serve her a cup of hot tea when I'd rather yell at her and walk away?"

"Let me ask you this," one of the men said. "Do you believe—at the core of who you are—that you love your wife?"

"I want to," Frank replied.

"Then you need quite literally to step into the truth of it. The actions that demonstrate love will then inform your belief. A change in your behavior will be your best chance at softening her heart, and your commitment to love will grow stronger as you put your decision to love into practice. Once you believe with your whole heart, then acting in love always becomes easier. Your passion will be reactivated, and the entire cycle will become more naturally regenerative.

"But first," and Frank would hear this message repeated time and again, "you're going to have to *choose* to believe."

So What

- So you say that you want your church to grow
- or you keep telling people you wish the men's ministry at your place of worship would develop some life
- or you confess to your pastor that you wish you were the kind of man who "had it in him" to invite others to church
- or maybe you find yourself disinterested during worship, unmotivated to pray, or completely disengaged from your "role" as a Christian when you're doing anything other than merely showing up at church

Go ahead and admit that you feel that way. There's no need to be discouraged. You basically have a passion deficit in your Christian experience.

The antidote for passionless faith is the willful application of belief. That is worth repeating to make sure we fully understand it: *The antidote for passionless faith is the willful application of belief.*

The Bottom Line

- Make the decision to believe. "Immediately the father of the child cried out, 'I believe; help my unbelief!'" (Mark 9:24).
- Step into that belief by engaging in belief-grounded actions. Begin each day with a devotion, pray several times during the day, tell someone about Jesus or invite them to worship, join a small group at church, read the Bible daily, serve in a mission- or service-oriented activity, and/or be a deliberately generous giver.
- Testify. Tell a friend about your decision to practice belief. Share it with your small group or class at church. Tell yourself by keeping a prayer journal or writing out personal devotions.
- Ask God, every day, for the gift of faith and the fullness of God's Spirit. Thank God for renewing you, even when you have a hard time feeling anything other than your own conviction.

Therefore, since we are justified by faith, we have peace with God through our Lord Jesus Christ, through whom we have obtained access to this grace in which we stand; and we boast in our hope of sharing the glory of God. And not only that, but we also boast in our sufferings, knowing that suffering produces endurance, and endurance produces character, and character produces hope, and hope does not disappoint us, because God's love has been poured into our hearts through the Holy Spirit that has been given to us (Rom. 5:1-5).

God's love, poured into our hearts through the Holy Spirit.

Let's Talk about It

Use these questions for personal reflection, in reading this book with a couple of friends, or for discussion as a study group in your faith community.

1. Would you describe yourself as a passionate Christian? Would anyone else describe you that way? What evidence would they cite in their rationale?

2. Share a situation when excitement overwhelmed you. (Watching a game? Being in love? Landing a job? The birth of a child?)

3. If someone asked you, "What are you passionate about?" or "What couldn't you live without?" what answers would come to mind?

4. Is it easy to include Jesus in the list you made for question 3? Your faith? Or would you—honestly—be stretching it a little to say, "Oh, yes, God! I was thinking about God the whole time!"

5. Read this scripture:

In all these things we are more than conquerors through him who loved us. For I am convinced that neither death, nor life, nor angels, nor rulers, nor things present, nor things to come, nor powers, nor height, nor depth, nor anything else in all creation, will be able to separate us from the love of God in Christ Jesus our Lord (Rom. 8:37-39).

    a. Does reading this scripture give you (as my wife would say) "chilly-bumps"? Why or why not?

    b. If you are not "convinced that neither death, nor life . . . can separate you from the love of God," then consider asking God to teach you how. If you do ask and you are serious, then hold on to your hat.

6. Are you committed to or at least interested in a life-charged faith? Share how you plan to claim the idea of passion in your own spiritual journey.

PRAYER: Sometimes we shy away from feelings and emotions, God, because we are afraid of giving up control. Instead of boundless enthusiasm for you, we present a guarded front and hide behind the carefully defined lines we have drawn. Give us the courage to erase those barriers; meet us at the edge of our passion; and draw us into a renewal of life. Infuse us with life-charged enthusiasm and delight for your way. Amen.

FOUR
CAPACITY

Only be strong and very courageous, being careful to act in accordance with all the law that my servant Moses commanded you; do not turn from it to the right hand or to the left, so that you may be successful wherever you go. This book of the law shall not depart out of your mouth; you shall meditate on it day and night, so that you may be careful to act in accordance with all that is written in it. For then you shall make your way prosperous, and then you shall be successful. I hereby command you: Be strong and courageous; do not be frightened or dismayed, for the LORD your God is with you wherever you go.

JOSHUA 1:7-9

Capacity: The ability to receive or contain; the maximum amount that can be contained; volume; the power to receive; actual or potential ability.

This is a book of ideas and, as such, is designed primarily for reading. You know, open to a page and you see nothing but words and punctuation; the emphasis is on the text. But I'd like you to imagine a big color photograph, pasted right here. This image will go a long way toward setting the stage, because the scene in my mind that gives rise to this chapter is vibrant, high-definition, and hard to describe using words alone.

I often project the picture I'm talking about on the wall when I'm out on the road speaking. The scene is a church fellowship hall, teeming with people attending a wedding reception. Many of the guests are dancing, their hands thrust up into the air, celebrating a key moment, doing the "Y.M.C.A." There is lots of laughter too, and if you look closely you can see numerous groupings at tables or standing, everyone in animated conversation.

I'm describing a still picture, not a video, so there's no sound track. Yet, somehow the photograph is alive with action and life. The image is not just full to bursting with a crowd of people, but the people are overflowing too, with vibrant enthusiasm and the evidence of life.

Underneath this slide, in bold print, I have placed the following statement: "Christian community tells the truth about the gospel."

That fellowship hall is bursting at the seams with life and promise. The physical space is being used to capacity and the spirits of the people are full in the same way. But, at the same time, they don't appear to be contained.

In his letter to Timothy, the apostle Paul talks about vibrant life:

> Command them to do good, to be rich in good deeds, and to be generous and willing to share. In this way they will lay up treasure for themselves as a firm foundation for the coming age, so that they may take hold of the life that is truly life (1 Tim. 6:18-19, NIV).

What a great description of the gospel! "The life that is truly life," or, "The life that is life indeed." Paul is suggesting—and the point becomes even more clear when we read the entire chapter (1 Timothy 6)—that what we tend to call "life," much of the time, really isn't.

That bears repeating: *What we tend to call life, much of the time, really isn't.*

The way we live together as a faith community communicates clearly what we believe. Maybe the slide should read this way: "The way we live and worship together (as a body of believers) is—like it or not—an honest commentary on the quality of gospel we preach and of our capacity for the life-charged life."

Fact is, the "life that really is life" speaks for itself.

Life that speaks for itself is a great idea. So let's grab hold of it.

Life-charged to Capacity

God promised Joshua success and prosperity (Josh. 1:7-9). So, right from the start we need to distinguish between what the Bible teaches about success and prosperity and the tendency of some folk to make the case that what God actually wants is for believers to live in bigger houses and drive newer cars (sometimes referred to as "the Gospel of Wealth"). The belief that God only wants us to have wealth is both a very narrow definition of prosperity and a tragically cynical view of success.

This divine invitation to "prosper" and "be successful" is the primary reason that the word *capacity* jumped out, time and again, when I pared the shortlist of life-charged words from twenty-plus to ten. The Bible, both Old and New Testaments, is stock full of stories about people—men and women—who responded to God's invitation to live to capacity and who tapped into the transformational power available for us when we live into the possibilities available by our being made in the "image of God."

When humankind was forced out of the garden of Eden, a system breakdown ensued that was in effect a disengagement from the true source of life. The result, according to the biblical narrative, was catastrophic. The continuing story of the Hebrew Bible, which finds its ultimate fulfillment in the life and invitation of Jesus as put forth by the Gospels, is the challenge by God to people of faith to live as if they truly are redeemed people. A huge part of how our lives can reflect that redemption is to move beyond half measures and into what Jesus described as life in all of its abundance (or fullness; see John 10:10).

This fullness, this abundance, this prosperity and success, has nothing to do with the accumulation of material trinkets and everything to do with living out our potentiality as God's beloved children.

9/11

Let's go back to this virtual PowerPoint show we're running in our imaginations, synchronized with the text. Let's turn our attention to another slide on the screen. This image is disturbing at first glance, but it strikes at the core of this conversation about capacity.

The picture I'm referring to was taken as the tragic events of September 11, 2001 (9/11), were unfolding. The photograph shows five men (two firemen and three others) as they emerge from the base of the World Trade Center, carrying the body of New York City Fire Department Chaplain Father Mychal F. Judge. Judge was in the lobby of the North Tower, helping victims, when the South Tower collapsed at 9:59 AM. He was killed by falling debris.

9/11 was perhaps the most difficult day in the recent history of our nation. Father Judge was a priest who died living out his faith, serving others with every ounce of faithfulness he could muster. He died while he was engaging life at capacity, as were the men carrying his body from the building. They represent vitality, courage, meaning, purpose, camaraderie, and action. This photograph captures life in all its fullness.

For me, this picture of absolute selflessness, of complete giving, of faith in the face of danger and the specter of almost certain death, represents the kind of abundance Jesus was referencing in John 10:10. These are the values and the passions of men who are living a life-charged life, which embody the kind of "success" and "prosperity" that God promised to Joshua (1:7-9).

Not Quite as Advertised

So let's be honest: difficult images like this one don't get much air time when televangelists tell their audiences that God wants them to prosper to the tune of a new Mercedes-Benz or to be comfortable in a first-class, leather-padded lifestyle with all the perks.

Christianity is too often advertised as the ticket to a comfortable, easy-going life. We're promised that when we are right with God life will be a breeze. A satisfying life is about what we can do to receive God's favor. Some preachers even talk about faithful Christians getting the best parking spaces or an upgrade to cushy comfort on the airplane or the best seats in the house when we only paid for tickets in the balcony. In addition, if we have enough faith our children will be well behaved, we'll be able to afford luxury items, we'll be healed from sickness, and everything will go well.

If we're not careful, we also apply the same shallow thinking to pleasure: we equate the good life with indolence and ease; we may go so far as to believe that God's blessing will result in a life without stress or hard work.

We eventually become so lost in this lie that our churches fail to ask anything substantial of their members. We make it easy to join and we try hard to cater to members' preferences because we want them to come back next week. We avoid offending people by not talking about giving, not asking for commitments, and not suggesting any kind of sacrificial anything.

So when we look around and we don't see too many men, it worries us. As a result, we lower the bar even further because we so much want them to like us. "Please don't leave our church. We won't ask you to do anything difficult. Joining is easy." Unfortunately, membership that is not difficult can also quite often become not important.

How do the values and passions of the typical church compare to the values and passions of the life-charged life? How can such a low-impact, undemanding gospel appeal to men whose values and passions seek the opportunity to engage life at a full-tilt, action demanding, "make-me-sweat-why-don't-you" pace? Where is the camaraderie that responds to a purpose and a cause that we'd willingly give our lives for because we follow this life-giving, life-demanding Jesus?

> But this I call to mind,
>   and therefore I have hope:
> The steadfast love of the LORD never ceases,
>   his mercies never come to an end;
> they are new every morning;
>   great is your faithfulness.
> "The LORD is my portion," says my soul,
>   "therefore I will hope in him."
>   Lamentations 3:21-24

Brain Power!

Many of us have heard the (unsubstantiated) theory that most humans use only a small portion of their mental faculties. Another popular factoid holds that after the human brain has grown for a few years, we start losing brain mass in response to aging, head injuries, ingesting the wrong substances, illness, and other reasons. Such a juxtaposition of theories raises the question about when the two graph lines might meet. *At what point,* we wonder, *will the "10 percent of the brain we use" become the "100 percent of the brain we have remaining?"*

Proven fact or mere speculation, the issue regarding how much of our brain that we utilize fails to address the more critical question, "How do we actually exercise those three pounds of grey matter from day to day?"

Capacity is not simply a question about ration, volume, or even usage. Take, for example, a piano. If a person played one note at a time, moving from left to right up the keyboard, it could be said that he or she used the entire instrument. Although technically true from a literal perspective, this statement is false when we consider the potential for doing so much more: a classical prelude by Chopin, *Rhapsody in Blue* by Gershwin, "Imagine" by John Lennon, or a complex rag by Scott Joplin. If we listen to any of the great composers, the phrase "using the entire keyboard" takes on a new level of meaning. Creativity can't be measured according to standard metrics, and the idea of capacity has as much to do with imagination as it has with storage or dimension.

Imagination and Capacity

Public school teachers will tell you that nothing discourages them more than mandatory, standards-based tests and the production-line approach to education that those tests lead to. One drawback to standardized assessments is the failure of punch cards to measure anything other than data that can be reduced to a binary code. Consequently, too many schools feel pressured to abandon creativity in favor of force-feeding facts that students can regurgitate on demand.

Earlier I referred to a study that documented the loss of creativity during the years of public schooling. Children enter kindergarten bursting with creativity but as they are cranked through the educational sausage machine their imaginations are systematically dampened until there's precious little originality remaining.

We can stuff our brains to the brim with information, but that's not the meaning of capacity in the life-charged life. The scriptures declare that we are created in the image of God. Capacity means connecting with the power source of light and creative life and living as beings created in the image of God. That means that light and life and creativity and hope and purpose reside in people and that how we live our lives should leave no doubt as to whose image we are created in.

The ability to live at capacity was lost when Adam and Eve hid among the trees (Genesis 3) and effectively sabotaged their relationship with God. That ability is the heart of the promise contained in a renewed, reconciled spiritual life that is reborn in Jesus and nurtured by the Holy Spirit.

To Capacity and Beyond. . . .

God designed each of us to live at capacity—or at least to live approaching capacity and pushing its limits because we were designed with much more in mind than the mediocrity of the uninspired. We are more likely to live in the beauty of our potential when we are in relationship with God. God puts us in touch with life, love, beauty, peace, goodness, and grace. Which is why we should strive to erase any distinctions between our life and our "spiritual" life. Eventually they will become one and the same, in much the same way that Adam and Eve walked with God in the cool of the afternoon in the garden.

Paul's words to the Galatians speak to the evidence of gospel in everyday life.

> The fruit of the Spirit is love, joy, peace, patience, kindness, generosity, faithfulness, gentleness, and self-control. There is no law against such things. And those who belong to Christ Jesus have crucified the flesh with its passions and desires. If we live by the Spirit, let us also be guided by the Spirit. Let us not become conceited, competing against one another, envying one another (Gal. 5:22-26).

Metanatural

Living to capacity is, in a very real sense, miraculous. God's plan brings us to places we otherwise could not have imagined. Rather than otherworldly or beyond the natural order, God achieves results that have always been intended for this amazing and wonderful life we've been given, written into the DNA of possibility from the dawn of creation. If we're living to capacity then what we call miracles can more accurately be described as "metanatural" rather than supernatural. To understand the idea of metanatural think

- extra
- more nearly comprehensive

- beyond what we can easily see as natural
- transcending the expected
- at a higher state of development
- pushing capacity

Supernatural presupposes that God is an outsider and works in ways outside of nature. Metanatural implies that God is not an outsider but that God is a natural fit for this life. God created this world with imagination and love and declared the work as "good." Our world was designed with the exact specifications to serve as the place where a natural relationship between the created and the Creator would take place. Experiencing God, given this understanding, becomes a crucial element of what it means to live in the natural world. God is not otherworldly; God is "metaworldly."

This means that we do the work of creation a disservice when we relegate God to the status of outsider or external reference point. And we do disservice to the intention of God's creative work when we conduct our lives in a manner that excludes the divine. A life lived in communion with God is therefore the most natural thing in the world, especially when we consider that we are created both in the image of God as well as for relationship with God.

Capacity Increases with Faith

Most discussions around the idea of capacity work with the assumptions not only that an organism (whether an individual or an organization) can grow to capacity but not beyond, but also that when we approach our capacity a kind of stasis sets in. "Operating at capacity" is interpreted as a signal that the growth phase is over.

But when we're talking about capacity in the context of the life-charged life, faith operates more like a water balloon. At first glance, a balloon looks to have room for a specific amount of water. If you measure the balloon—length, breadth, depth—and then do the math, you can determine the exact amount of water it will hold. The balloon is, for the record, a container that will hold a fixed amount. But that fact remains true only so long as the balloon is not actually being used. The instant you begin to pour water into a balloon, everything changes. The balloon will stretch in response to the weight of the water, which, lo and behold, increases its capacity. The more water you pour in, the more the balloon opens up for more (within limits, of course). The point is, the carrying capacity of the balloon expands in response to the experience of its *being filled*.

Our spiritual capacity is like that as well. God wants to fill us to capacity and beyond. When God pours in life it is untapped potential that's now released. It is promise newly created, as we open ourselves up to more control and direction from the Holy Spirit. Are we guilty of simply talking about insight or recognition of what was there all along?

Capacity encompasses more than being life-charged; capacity is metanatural. Capacity involves something that is dynamic in the context of the life-charged life, which is why capacity is a natural choice as one of our life-charged words.

The Bottom Line

- We were created explicitly by God to live in a relationship with God.
- We will never approach our capacity unless we engage in that relationship.

- As we approach the limits of our understanding of capacity, God will add to what is possible.
- Jesus said to him, "If you are able!—All things can be done for the one who believes." Immediately the father of the child cried out, "I believe; help my unbelief!" (Mark 9:23-24).
- When we are willing for God to use us at capacity (and beyond), then everything we do becomes charged with extra life.

Let's Talk about It

Use these questions for personal reflection, in reading this book with a couple of friends, or for discussion as a study group in your faith community.

1. What is your assessment of how you live in relationship to capacity? What room is there for an extra charge of life-charged life?
2. What Bible-story character do you think of as one who lived at capacity? Take a moment to look up the story. What can you/we learn from this hero of the faith?
3. Discuss the idea of metanatural (page 65). In what ways do you see God working naturally in the world?
4. Think about "the life that is truly life" (1 Tim. 6:19-20). How does the illustration from the 9/11 tragedy make sense in terms of capacity?
5. Imagine how Joshua would respond to the idea that a person of faith should be rewarded with an easy, comfortable life. Write a dialogue between yourself and Joshua discussing the issue.

6. What is one element of your life where you feel challenged to live at capacity?

PRAYER: We were created for such wondrous things, Lord. May we willingly invite your Spirit to dwell in us and to lift us beyond the limits of what we imagine. As life-charged followers of Jesus, living at capacity, we can change the world and lead others into a deeper experience of purpose and peace. Amen.

FIVE
SCRIPTURE

I seek you with all my heart;
   do not let me stray from your commands.
I have hidden your word in my heart
   that I might not sin against you.
Praise be to you, LORD;
   teach me your decrees.

PSALM 119:10-12 (NIV)

Scripture: The sacred writings of the Bible.

Logos: A ground, order, knowledge; the animating principle of divinity; the Word incarnate.

Ground: Foundation, basis, the earth beneath our feet, what we stand on, the source of gravitational pull, a basis for belief and action.

At thirty-five years of age, Kemper Stevens owns so many commitments—all of them good—that his life is ultrabusy from dawn until dusk. Married, with two extra-lively elementary-aged children, he teaches school, referees soccer, and enjoys doing "church stuff" with his wife.

You'd think he had enough to do in the mornings without including a devotion in his busy day. Instead, without fail and within moments of getting out of bed, Kemper picks up his smart phone (the alarm of which has recently awakened him) and checks his email (one specific email, to be precise). And there, sure enough, Kemper finds the devotional message sent directly to his address during the night via subscription.

Kemper does three things with the devotional. First, he reads the paragraph-length scripture selection, taking his time and letting the words and the ideas sink in. Then he reads the short meditation. Last, he memorizes the key verse selected by that day's author and writes it on a small card, which he places in his wallet. All in all, the commitment takes about five minutes of uninterrupted concentration.

A little later, while he's brushing his teeth before heading out to work, Kemper repeats the verse several times in his head so the scripture is well and truly memorized.

"'Do not judge, so that you may not be judged. For with the judgment you make you will be judged, and the measure you give will be the measure you get.' Matthew seven, the first two verses," he'll recite to his wife when he's finished. "I'm going to remember that one today when I'm driving to work."

Or, "Listen to this, kids: 'God has sent the Spirit of his Son into our hearts, crying, "Abba! Father!" So you are no longer a slave but a child, and if a child then also an heir, through God.' That's Galatians four, six through seven. Now isn't that something to think about!"

Powerful Stuff

Scripture is a significant and powerful life-charged word. Consider the numerous passages in Genesis 1 where God literally speaks creation into being: "Then God said . . . ," "Then God said . . . ," "Then God said. . . ." Time and again it is God's Word that creates life.

The initial verses of John's Gospel echo the thought of Genesis. "In the beginning was the Word, and the Word was with God, and the Word was God. . . . What has come into being in him was life, and the life was the light of all people" (John 1:1, 3-4).

God's Word has literally created, animated, and sustained life since the beginning of time or even since before the beginning of time (if we can use a word such as *before* in relation to a setting outside the boundary of time).

Scripture serves not only as the written record of God's relationship with people but also as a constant source of light and life by virtue of its intrinsic authority and incisive truth. In a sense, the Spirit of God literally inhabits Holy Scripture. So when we allow scripture to take up residence in our conscious and our subconscious thoughts, we become hardwired into a quality of light and life that is unavailable from any other practice.

Logos: The Word

Logos, as a word, has taken quite a journey through history. The journey started in the discipline of philosophy, where *logos* initially referred to "a ground," essentially a basis or a starting point for organizing a logical argument. Greek philosophers used the term to talk about an animating, divine principle that pervades the universe. The writer of John's Gospel understood Logos ("the Word") as the principle through which everything is made, and

Jesus as the incarnation of Logos, literally, the Word (the ground) made flesh. The bottom line is that the primary way in which we are introduced to God is through Jesus and the most important resource that we have to know Jesus is the collection of sacred writings contained in the Bible.

We cannot deny that something of the divine principle, the Logos, is contained in the actual words of the Bible, that it is not so much captured in those words as it is revealed by them. The Bible's authority must not and cannot be ascribed to human means. The Bible speaks truth and life and light into our experience in ways that lie beyond the scope of our understanding. It is as if the Bible is a portal into the spiritual world, an entry point into the consciousness of God.

Life-charged Words

Most of us enjoy some exposure to reading. Some of us read primarily for fun, others read to learn, and there are those who read for the sheer pleasure of consuming great literature. Certainly many of us read as a means of staying connected to culture.

Personally, I try to vary my reading: I will reward myself for completing something difficult (yet beneficial) by reading a couple of lightweight spy novels or an absorb-in-one-sitting mystery. My wife, Rebekah, on the other hand, is more conscientious, balancing her pile of spiritual resources with books and magazines on gardening and home improvement.

Interestingly, when we recently compared notes, we found that both of us have been spending more and more time reading the Bible.

"There's something going on with the scriptures," Rebekah said. "The text is increasingly alive and vital. The Bible is a living message from God. The words are two to four thousand years old, it was written in distant lands and extinct cultures, and it addresses situations that were unique to those times and places. Yet it is still animated with life; it remains relevant; it is more real than the morning newspaper. The scriptures seem to hold a sense of life that transcends the limitations of language and the decay of time."

Jesus, speaking in the Temple, put the idea this way: "Heaven and earth will pass away, but my words will not pass away" (Luke 21:33).

A Portal to the Kingdom

> So again Jesus said to them, "Very truly, I tell you, I am the gate for the sheep. All who came before me are thieves and bandits; but the sheep did not listen to them. I am the gate. Whoever enters by me will be saved, and will come in and go out and find pasture. The thief comes only to steal and kill and destroy. I came that they may have life, and have it abundantly" (John 10:7-10).

Two carpenters were installing a new front door in a home. After the prep work had been done, one of the men stood in the middle of the garden with the new door assembly while his colleague fetched some tools from their trailer. The man holding the door, standing directly in front of the opening, looked as if he were about to step through and disappear—like a character from the Chronicles of Narnia—into a parallel reality.

Hold that image in your mind's eye, because we'll come back to it in a little while.

Entry Points

One weekend at a men's conference somewhere on the West Coast, the leader asked the group to list the critical factors that might come into play whenever they encounter profound spiritual experiences. Another way of phrasing this question (thinking about the man holding the door in the middle of the garden) would be, "What have been your entry points into the kingdom of God?" The men responded with a variety of answers, which I have rephrased as questions in the following list:

- Is it prayer?
- Or great preaching?
- Maybe uplifting music?
- What about community?
- How about a guy with a door in the middle of your yard?
- Are you at church?
- In conversation with your small group?
- Reaching out in mission?
- Praying for a friend in need?
- Attending a conference?
- Leading a workshop or a retreat?
- When you are with other men and speaking openly about your faith?
- If none of the above, then describe what happens when you're simply telling your story.

Clearly, each of these elements has a part to play. But one important ingredient is missing from the list, the one that serves as the common denominator for most of the deep spiritual moments any of us experience. That ingredient is the Word of God. Men who experience a deep spiritual life are unfailingly captivated by the Bible.

Captivated by Design

"Unfailingly captivated by the Bible." As a writer, I enjoy the privilege of having a dedicated reading time almost every day. More and more, my natural choice has been to use this time to go back to the Bible and to open myself to the Word of God.

Bible study can be like praying and reading at the same time. If we pray prior to opening God's Word, first asking God to be present with us, to guide us, and to teach us, then we invariably will learn something both wonderful and new.

Even before offering a prayer, spending a few minutes in simple meditation can help to set the stage. Meditation can serve as a kind of the preprayer prayer, a getting ready to be ready. Meditation, as a spiritual practice, enables us to slow down, quiet down, concentrate, and settle into a place where we can be acutely aware of the presence of God before beginning any kind of a conversation.

Beginning Bible reading with meditation is a no-brainer. When we meditate, we disprove the unhelpful supposition that, "If God is already with us, we need not go looking." Not that any need exists for doubt concerning the promise of God's constant presence. But more than one person has commented, "God could be tap dancing on my desk and I probably wouldn't notice if I didn't first take the trouble to settle down and open my eyes"! Meditation is not so much looking for God as it is opening the shutters on our hearts, clearing our eyes, and putting on our best listening ears.

The Gate

Jesus is the gate. (See again John 10:7-10.)

- Jesus said people can and do literally "come in and go out" through him.

- Jesus is the way.
- Through Jesus we find pasture, nourishment for our souls, and, ultimately, abundant life.
- Jesus is the Logos, the Word(s) made flesh.
- Jesus is the Living Word.
- Jesus is the animation of the Word.

But what, where, and how is our gateway to Jesus? Each of us meets Jesus in many ways and in many places, but it is even more true to say that we meet Jesus most consistently in the Bible via our encounters with God's Word.

Let's get back to the guy we left standing in the middle of the garden, looking as if he is about to step through the frame and enter a parallel universe, a portal into another world. Cool image, right? Well, that's exactly what getting immersed in scripture does for us. God's Word is our most powerful connecting point to Jesus, and Jesus is the Living Word.

So scripture provides the best gateway into the kingdom of God. The Bible is our passport to spiritual consciousness. We can, as Jesus said, go in and come out again. But those who enter in and grow spiritually often find that they will, intentionally, stay in.

We must begin to inhabit God's Word, which becomes a life-charged kingdom experience.

More Than a Priority

We noted earlier that the word *logos* not only refers to the Bible and to Jesus but was first used in Greek philosophy to refer to "the ground," the basis or the starting point for an argument. Anything that has any substance or staying power must be rooted or grounded in something unshakable. In that regard, scripture can be seen as the ground we stand on in terms of faith.

Successful organizations often refer to the pillars they are built on, a series of fundamental priorities, principles, or values that express or support everything else they intend to achieve. The YMCA, for example, lists its pillars as "Youth Development, Healthy Living, and Social Responsibility."

As individuals, we too build our personal philosophy on pillars, whether we realize it or not. If asked, we may spell out our formal or informal mission statements, and we often reference God as "one of my priorities" or even "my top priority in life."

Dallas Cowboys coach Tom Landry often said God came first, then family and football. New York Jets quarterback Tim Tebow echoed that sentiment in a 2012 interview with *Good Morning America* host Robin Roberts.

Those may be convincing sound bites, but I'm inclined to think that the God we serve does not want to be a priority or even the *top* priority, that God has no interest in being included on any kind of list. Instead, especially if we're interested in living a life-charged life, then God must be *the very ground that we stand on.*

The Very Ground We Stand On

Let's repeat the previous idea. God has no interest in being included on any kind of a list. God as "just one more priority" in a person's life makes about as much sense as the popular but flawed idea expressed by the "God is my copilot" bumper sticker. Can you imagine the conversation when God is offered that position? "You want me as your *co*pilot? Really? Are you serious? You might as well ask me to leave the cockpit!"

God uses holy scripture not only to help keep us steady but also to keep us grounded. And not merely grounded but rooted. Being rooted in God's Word is a great way to make sure we are planted in God, so that God's Word can work on us. Luckily for us, scripture tends to do its own pruning. "Indeed, the word of God is living and active, sharper than any two-edged sword, piercing until it divides soul from spirit, joints from marrow; it is able to judge the thoughts and intentions of the heart" (Heb. 4:12).

Standing on the Promises

The old gospel hymn declares that believers stand on the promises of God ("Standing on the Promises," Russell Kelso Carter, 1886). Many of us have heard the quip that plays off this hymn, "There are not enough church members standing on the promises; too many of them are simply sitting on the premises." But let's think of the following twist on the idea. When scripture is the very ground that we stand on, then we're not standing on the promises so much as "living in the promise."

There's an inspiring New Testament passage that suggests that every promise articulated throughout the length and breadth of the biblical narrative is fulfilled in Jesus:

> As surely as God is faithful, our word to you has not been "Yes and No." For the Son of God, Jesus Christ, whom we proclaimed among you, Silvanus and Timothy and I, was not "Yes and No"; but in him it is always "Yes." For in him every one of God's promises is a "Yes." For this reason it is through him that we say the "Amen," to the glory of God (2 Cor. 1:18-20).

The NIV translates verse 20 this way: "For no matter how many promises God has made, they are 'Yes' in Christ."

For the life-charged follower of Jesus, scripture is both assurance and promise.

My Grandma Lily certainly believed in promise, and when I was a child she used a simple game to help me and my brother establish scripture as a life-charged concept in our lives. I don't remember exactly how often we played this game, but I'd like to think it was the first thing we did every time we visited at her home and later at her apartment (which was attached to our family home in the south of England).

My grandma owned a treasure we knew as "Grandma's promise box," a small, carefully made box with a close-fitting lid, stuffed with hundreds of tightly wound scrolls of parchment paper. Soon after we would arrive, my brother and I would ask to see the promise box or Grandma would suggest we get it. One of us would fetch the box, take off the lid, and pick up the pair of ivory-handled tweezers from inside. When we removed the lid, we could see only a pattern of circles, each parchment standing upright and each containing a separate promise from the Bible. Then Grandma would say, "Pick a promise, children," and we'd take turns doing so.

I'll never forget the sense of anticipation. It was as if light were leaking from the tightly wrapped scrolls, and we'd release that radiance into our lives when we read the precious text.

Among the numerous verses—all of course in the King James Version—I remember these:

- "There is no fear in love; but perfect love casteth out fear" (1 John 4:18).
- "But my God shall supply all your need according to his riches in glory by Christ Jesus" (Phil. 4:19).
- "For the LORD is good; his mercy is everlasting; and his truth endureth to all generations" (Psalm 100:5).
- "God is our refuge and strength, a very present help in trouble" (Psalm 46:1).

- "Peace I leave with you, my peace I give unto you: not as the world giveth, give I unto you. Let not your heart be troubled, neither let it be afraid" (John 14:27).

My brother and I would each read our verse, one per visit, and Grandma would talk a bit about what it meant. Then she'd help us memorize the scripture before we left.

We may not have memorized every promise held in Grandma's promise box, but the ones we did learn certainly equipped my brother and me to leave Grandma's presence charged with the life that can only come from God, speaking directly into our hearts, via the scripture.

What an amazing gift, not only to have been charged with a promise every time we spent a couple of hours at Grandma's home but also to develop a life-long habit of reading scripture in anticipation of learning God's promises for us. My memory is that I have lived my life less from the perspective of "standing on those promises" from God's Word and more from the perspective of "living in the promise," the promise of a life animated from the God-breathed logos of scripture.

God-Breathed

All Scripture is God-breathed and is useful for teaching, rebuking, correcting and training in righteousness, so that the servant of God may be thoroughly equipped for every good work (2 Tim. 3:16-17, NIV).

Don't you love the translation "God-breathed" in 2 Timothy 3:16-17? The language carries a powerful image of God the Creator transforming inanimate ink and paper with spiritual life, imparting the breath of heaven through God's own words.

And the picture the scripture paints is no exaggeration: scripture heals, scripture challenges, scripture trains, scripture equips, and scripture inspires. God's Word brings us into the presence of God and introduces us to the character of God with more reliability than any other resource that's available to us as deliberate followers of the Way of Jesus.

Application

Here is a life-charged, God-breathed promise: if we do what is necessary to make the holy scripture the ground that we stand on, then God-breathed life will likewise animate both our faith journey and our day-to-day lives. In fact, the two concepts will cease to be separate. Our everyday life will become our spiritual life; the two will be one and the same.

> Happy are those
>   who do not follow the advice of the wicked,
> or take the path that sinners tread,
>   or sit in the seat of scoffers;
> but their delight is in the law of the LORD,
>   and on his law they meditate day and night.
> They are like trees
>   planted by streams of water,
> which yield their fruit in its season,
>   and their leaves do not wither.
> In all that they do, they prosper.
>   Psalm 1:1-3

The Bottom Line

So where do we go from here? Allowing scripture to become a life-charged word in our experience requires a few deliberate steps. If we make the decision and take the time to start the ball rolling, then God will add the charge of life.

- Make an honest assessment: how often in a given week do you take time to read the Bible? Make a promise to God that from this time forward you will "treasure your word in my heart, so that I may not sin against you" (Ps. 119:11).
- Think about how you might meditate prior to reading God's Word. You might practice a minute of silence before you read, then ask God to prepare your heart to learn and to grow.
- Consider joining a Bible-study group at your church or inviting some friends to join you in a weekly Bible-discussion group. Compile a list of people you might invite to join. Contemplate what some of your hopes and what some of your reservations for such an experience might be.
- Allow God's Word time and space to work its way into your consciousness.

To conclude this life-charged chapter, take a few moments to do the following exercise (note that I'm not calling it homework!): Find seven promises in scripture that speak to your heart. Write them out on seven index cards. Fold them neatly, put them in a sandwich bag, and take a different card out to memorize each day over the next week. You won't quite have a promise box, but it will be effective just the same.

Let's Talk about It

Use these questions for personal reflection, in reading this book with a couple of friends, or for discussion as a study group in your faith community.

1. Read Psalm 1 aloud. If you're in a group, read it in unison. Now talk about the idea of the tree and the water. Has God's Word ever nourished you like that?
2. How does Psalm 1 speak to your current life circumstance? How is God speaking to you today?
3. Tell the story of how you acquired your current copy of the Bible.
4. Have you ever considered a "read through the Bible in a year" devotional guide? Talk about the idea with this group or a friend.
5. If you had the opportunity to share one passage of scripture with the whole world, what passage would you pick? Why? If you can't think of a passage, then make a point of doing some Bible reading this week!

PRAYER: God who animates the words of scripture by your Spirit, we invite you to sit with us as we learn to study your word and hide its promises in our hearts. We want to become like trees planted by the water and grow as life-charged followers of the Way. Amen.

SIX
HOLINESS

Like obedient children, do not be conformed to the desires that you formerly had in ignorance. Instead, as he who called you is holy, be holy yourselves in all your conduct; for it is written, "You shall be holy, for I am holy."

1 PETER 1:14-16

O worship the LORD in the beauty of holiness.

PSALM 96:9 (KJV)

Holiness: Different, set aside, unique. The state of being hallowed, or consecrated to God; the worship of God; sacredness. Pureness of heart, light, goodness, godliness, blessedness.

The occasion was a late-summer Wednesday evening, and the conversation at Main Street Church turned serious. Twenty-two men had gathered for a small group Bible study. They were there to talk about holiness and its relationship to the life-charged life.

"I'm uncomfortable with the whole idea of holiness," one forty-year-old said. "I thought 'holiness' was holy-roller talk or something from the Old Testament. You know, something we don't need to worry about any more. How can there be any life-charged element to guilt?"

"I don't think holiness is about guilt so much as opportunity," one thirty-something offered. "But I would like to talk about how we go about addressing the idea in practical terms. How on earth can I possibly be holy? How can someone like me approach God, knowing how I am? I agree that a little more holiness is precisely what I need if I'm going to grow from this point forward, but I can't imagine how I can get there."

The shift in conversation was no surprise when it came. First, it was obvious there'd be some talk about law versus grace: "What's with the legalism?" Especially from the guys who struggle to stay connected with their faith walk. But several other men in the room were used to being more open. They tended to be hard on themselves, yes; but at the same time they were ready to grow and to let the Spirit lead.

"First let's talk about what holiness might mean in our regular lives as men who are committed to living our faith out loud," the leader said. "Then we'll conclude by addressing the 'how' part of the equation. But right now I want to let my favorite scripture about holiness sit on your hearts and minds and percolate a little."

He read aloud: "'Now the Lord is the Spirit,' Paul wrote to his friends in the Corinthian church, 'and where the Spirit of the Lord is, there is freedom. And all of us, with unveiled faces, seeing the glory of the Lord as though reflected in a mirror, are being transformed into the same image from one degree of glory to another; for this comes from the Lord, the Spirit'" [2 Cor. 3:17-18].

"One degree of glory to another" is indeed quite a tall order. But we'll come back to that later.

Holiness Is Not an Outdated Model

Holiness, for the purposes of this discussion, has to do with how evidence of God rubs off on us as followers of Jesus. Or, put another way, it's the measure of how authentically we shine. In Philippians 2, the apostle Paul suggested that we be "blameless and innocent, children of God without blemish in the midst of a crooked and perverse generation, in which you shine like stars in the world" (v. 15). Holiness as a standard is a difficult concept to articulate, so we often dismiss it as archaic or discount the idea as a legalistic approach to living.

However, a conversation about holiness is exactly what we need, especially if we truly are motivated to talk about what it means to live a faith-based life that moves us beyond the realm of the mundane and into the territory we're beginning to understand as life-charged.

We could possibly find a more contemporary word or take steps to smooth out the sharper edges of the idea so that it might play more easily to the twenty-first century audience. But taking an honest look at holiness, straight up, is unavoidable if we want to latch on to life in the way that our discussion so far suggests.

Holiness Is Improbable, Out of Character, and Unnatural

Let's face it, holiness probably doesn't come naturally to anyone. Have you ever known a man who could walk into a room and be greeted like this?

- "Wow, you've got some pureness of heart going on, mister!" or,
- "Goodness, the light of godliness sure is strong around you today!"

Instead, what we expect from the guys we hang around with is quite the opposite. Men in our society, unless otherwise coached, tend toward the profane, the ungodly, the worldly, the earthy, and, in general, the less refined. We're taught to "go for the gusto," not for the arts. No offense.

Come to think of it, I'd wager that none of us needs to make any special effort to act selfish, wrong, insensitive, impatient, or uncooperative or that we have to try very hard to make a situation worse. No, of course not. We're men, and we're naturally gifted that way!

By a show of hands, who gets up in the morning, goes about their day, and thinks, *What can I do to upset my wife over the next few hours?* or, *I've got to think hard on my way home from work so I can make sure to ruin the entire evening by saying something insensitive over dinner.* Unfortunately, for many of us these experiences come without any effort at all—almost like a talent! They are predilections rooted in our nature and, if we're not careful, unholiness tends to rule the way we live on a day-by-day basis.

However, when I say that unholiness is rooted in our nature, I'm acknowledging that our actions grow out of patterns of behavior we have learned from our culture, patterns that go against the fundamental design of being fully human or fully engaging the life-charged life. I'm not arguing that God created us as better suited for lives of unholiness, only that we are so unaccustomed to living an authentic relationship with God that we more likely default to the profane.

Holiness = Opportunity, Not Obligation

The truth is that holiness, living as if grace is a reality and not merely a promise, should be more properly understood as an opportunity than as an obligation. Sin is what's unnatural. The hard reality, though, is that such a beautiful state of affairs (holiness) often leads to frustration when we try to put it into practice.

Paul writes of his struggle with that same challenge. Even following his dramatic conversion and lifetime of service, the tendency to act in certain unholy ways never seemed to relinquish its hold. He describes the situation as a war raging inside him.

> I find it to be a law that when I want to do what is good, evil lies close at hand. For I delight in the law of God in my inmost self, but I see in my members another law at war with the law of my mind, making me captive to the law of sin that dwells in my members. Wretched man that I am! Who will rescue me from this body of death? (Rom. 7:21-24).

A Call to Victory

The call to holiness is a call to victory, a call to victory specifically in terms of the ongoing struggle to draw attention to the truth about God, through the evidence of the way we live.

But this is not a battle we can win by our own efforts or by applying a hearty dose of self-control. Paul goes on to say that we absolutely must involve the Spirit or we are dead in the water: "To set the mind on the flesh is death, but to set the mind on the Spirit is life and peace" (Rom. 8:6).

A Spiritual Boost

Holiness provides a kind of "spiritual boost" for this life-charged life. On our own we're reduced to setting out on a valiant effort to engage life; but without God's help, our effort becomes an effort based on the force of our own will and our need to "tough it out" on our own. Thus it is doomed to fail.

We might, for example, set out to "live at capacity" (*capacity* being one of our life-charged words). Living at capacity is a worthy goal, but we need forward movement in terms of holiness to hook us up with the power necessary to operate at (and beyond) our full capacity.

Basically, holiness is power, and in order to live life-charged lives we need that power. The life-charged life isn't a vague possibility apart from a deep, rich, abiding relationship with the Creator who designed us. But both the scope and the reach of that relationship are seriously hobbled if we neglect the life-charged concept of holiness. Living in holiness is like removing the gunk, the rust, and the dirt that hinders the spark from our spiritual contacts from igniting.

Beyond the Old Testament?

It can be tempting to dismiss concepts such as purity by relegating the idea to archaic religious structures or by saying that holiness is irrelevant because nobody needs the rituals of Old Testament priests any more.

That purification was an Old Covenant obligation, necessary when a person desired to approach God, is undeniable. And Christians believe that Jesus moved heaven and earth to place us beyond the reach of such requirements. But we need to take care not to throw the proverbial baby out with the bath water. Too many of us act as if holiness has no relevance for our lives today. Nothing could be further from the truth. Granted, certain aspects of holiness as taught by the Old Testament (for example, purification) are no longer seen as mandatory, but that doesn't mean that the entire concept of holiness has disappeared.

Holiness is a life-charged concept and a powerful tool because, as a natural response to the realization that we all receive God's grace and need do nothing to earn the right to stand in the presence of God, holiness becomes a response to the good news and thus serves as an effective agent of change and a potent witness to life.

Drawing Attention to the Truth about God

Holiness is at play when people draw attention to the truth about God simply by being. Let's check some examples:

When Moses came down from the mountain, having spent some quality time with God, his face was literally shining. That's how obvious it was that the great leader had been in God's presence.

> Moses came down from Mount Sinai. As he came down from the mountain with the two tablets of the covenant in his hand, Moses did not know that the skin of his face shone because he had been talking with God (Exod. 34:29).

Saint Francis of Assisi took a novice out for a day of preaching the gospel. As they left Assisi, they helped a farmer move his cart; down the road they talked with a merchant and listened to his problems; around noon they shared their meal with a hungry beggar; soon after lunch they prayed with a sick woman; on their way back, they helped a woman carry her heavy load. When they returned to the monastery at dark, the novice commented that the day was gone and they hadn't preached to anyone. "My son," Francis responded, "we've been sharing the gospel all day long."

Perhaps you know someone who is soft-spoken and generally works behind the scenes. He always looks out for the interests of other people and is the first to serve. With or without words, the people around him are spiritually nourished by being in his presence.

Another man may be successful in business yet humble. He doesn't curse, he always speaks encouragingly, he spends a lot of his day in silent prayer, and he leads by example. He loves his wife with genuine affection and is generous to a fault. People are drawn to this man, and many of them remark that he reminds them of Jesus.

Now let's check out some negative-examples:

Imagine a man who makes a lot of noise about being a Christian and who tells people he is totally committed to Christ. But he yells at his wife, puts her down constantly, berates her publicly, and tells their children it's her fault they might be getting a divorce.

A well-known evangelist speaks publicly about his "pure heart" and publicly condemns those he considers immoral. When he is arrested with child pornography in his possession, he makes the gospel he proclaimed a very loud and very public falsehood.

A member of a church loses his temper on the golf course and frequently curses during his game, pretty much every time he plays. The men he plays with may have been interested in a life of faith. Now they can't see the point.

A man expresses a serious desire about connecting with God on a deeper level. He attends church on occasion and has been thinking about joining a men's study group. But he can't seem to make any progress in terms of moving forward spiritually. Might this be connected in any way to his tendency to view trash, to use foul language, to enjoy sharing dirty jokes with his friends, and to excuse this behavior by claiming that it honestly doesn't matter?

Deliberately making holiness a part of our experience can go a long way toward the objective of telling the truth about God through our being. Holiness may take the pressure off of us in terms of verbally sharing the story, because we are already sharing the story to the extent that we are living holy lives.

How in the World?

Let's go back to the issue stated at the beginning of this chapter, the one the men's group discussed before the guys went home that evening. "We agree that a little more holiness is what we need if we're going to grow from this point forward, but I can't imagine how we can get there."

As I see it, moving from a profane life to a life-charged holiness (let alone "from glory into glory") is essentially a twofold process: First, it requires committing to the deliberate practice of spending time in the presence of God. Second, and in equal measure, we must choose to apply specific and deliberate changes to the way that we live and what we allow ourselves to encounter.

Spending Time with God

Earlier we noted the example of Moses, who was literally radiant because he'd been in the presence of God. His radiance unnerved the people, so they asked him to wear a veil and to hide his face. Paul referred to that same story in the passage from 2 Corinthians 3, which the men's group at Main Street Church were asked to think about vis-à-vis holiness.

Paul told the story of Moses to illustrate the fact that, because of Jesus, nothing, not even a veil, needs to come between Christians and the presence of God.

Seeing the glory of the Lord as though reflected in a mirror, [we] are being transformed into the same image from one degree of glory to another (2 Cor 3:17-18).

That's heady stuff.

Heady or not, this passage outlines an amazing principle we can tap into. Spending time with Jesus can be like looking into a mirror, except that in this mirror the image changes from that of our unholy selves into the image of Christ.

To put it simply: spend time with Jesus. The move toward life-charged holiness always begins in the presence of Jesus.

Making the Needed Changes

Perhaps more challenging, it is essential that we make deliberate and well-considered changes in the realm of our actual behavior, which captures the meaning behind Paul's "working out our salvation" passage in Philippians.

Therefore, my beloved, just as you have always obeyed me, not only in my presence, but much more now in my absence, work out your own salvation with fear and trembling; for it is God who is at work in you, enabling you both to will and to work for his good pleasure (Phil. 2:12-13).

The life-charged life is no free ride; it turns out to be much more meaningful and engaging than that, which is why Paul could say, "Wretched man that I am" (Rom. 7:24) in contrast to what he could be.

Many of us can corroborate from our experience that the Spirit tends to become involved to the extent that we make deliberate efforts ourselves. Not that holiness gets any easier as we go along, so much as the growing sense that God reinforces our personal faithfulness with the gift of spiritual strength.

> The law of the Spirit of life in Christ Jesus has set you free from the law of sin and of death. For God has done what the law, weakened by the flesh, could not do: by sending his own Son in the likeness of sinful flesh, and to deal with sin, he condemned sin in the flesh, so that the just requirement of the law might be fulfilled in us, who walk not according to the flesh but according to the Spirit (Rom. 8:2-4).

In terms of personal discipline, here's a partial list of what many faithful men have learned when it comes to stacking the deck in favor of holiness. Note: any activity that fails to honor God is antilife and antiholiness.

1. Begin each day (without exception) with a personal devotional time.
2. Initiate a daily Bible-reading regimen.
3. Ask a trusted friend to pray for you (and sometimes with you) as you deal with areas where you need to initiate change.
4. Eliminate profanity from your vocabulary.
5. Monitor your online and television-viewing habits; eliminate any practice that fails to honor God.
6. Employ the "unseen guest" principle; visually imagine Jesus being with you at the golf course, at the table, at the computer, riding in your car, or wherever you are.
7. Attend worship on a regular basis.
8. In place of unholy practices that you eliminate, add activities that advance holiness. Listen to praise music in the car, for example, rather than filling your mind with that

raunchy radio show (which you'd be uncomfortable sharing with Jesus anyhow).

Living Evidence of Holiness

I became [the gospel's] servant according to God's commission that was given to me for you, to make the word of God fully known, the mystery that has been hidden throughout the ages and generations but has now been revealed to his saints. To them God chose to make known how great among the Gentiles are the riches of the glory of this mystery, which is Christ in you, the hope of glory (Col. 1:25-27).

"Christ in you, the hope of glory" is the holiness equation!

The fullness of God, Paul writes, was once a mystery that was hidden away. Interestingly, the element that makes this mystery so rich is the same element that now makes it so accessible, which is "Christ in us, the hope of glory."

One thing that I love about Jesus and about the Christmas message is its accessibility—the simple story of a baby, vulnerable and dependent on the fortunes of a young refugee family. Fundamentally, the message of Christmas can be summed up as "God made accessible," God without pretense and without the buffer of contrived religiosity.

The baby Jesus grew up, became a man, shared the essentials of what it means to live the life-charged life, discipled a small group of followers, and then left the balance of the story to us.

Which is why Paul can say that the glory and the richness of the mystery is how Christ becomes evident in the way that we live. Both Jesus and Paul made it clear that the hope of glory is communicated—or not—via the evidence we present, by living the gospel out loud.

By living the gospel out loud we become

- billboards for God's grace
- emissaries of promise
- evidence that the mystery is no longer hidden
- God's big PR gamble
- an advertisement for the validity (or not) of this "new and living way" Jesus came to set in motion.

Today I recommend a contemplative frame of mind and spirit. Think about the essentials; think about Jesus.

The Bottom Line

Applied holiness is like tapping into power.

Among the life-charged words, *holiness* offers an almost measurable potency. Holiness leads to a visible shift in terms of our influence and the power to effect positive change in this world.

- Holiness is drawing attention to the truth about God simply by being.
- Imagine the world in which you live (your family, work, friends) being changed by your personal holiness.
- Imagine your life becoming so attuned to the Spirit of God that people come away from spending time with you blessed and restored.
- Imagine the charge of life that will emanate from your day-to-day living because holiness is now a life-charged priority.
- Holiness involves the simple decision to spend more time in the presence of God and to allow the encounter to change you.

Let's Talk about It

Use these questions for personal reflection, in reading this book with a couple of friends, or for discussion as a study group in your faith community.

1. How much time do you intentionally spend in the presence of Jesus each day?
2. Discuss how you might go about increasing the amount of time you deliberately spend in the presence of Jesus.
3. Make two lists:
   - regular behaviors that serve to move you in the direction of holiness; and
   - behaviors that work against holiness or promote the unholy elements in your life.
4. Think of one or two individuals you know (either personally or by reputation) who "draw attention to the truth about God simply by being." Try to describe what gives their witness such power.
5. In what ways do you feel that the priority of holiness would add a life-charged aspect to the way that you live?

PRAYER: O God, when we think of the word *holy*, we think of you and we're reminded that we have been created in your image. We're also reminded that you call on us to honor that image through the way we live. We want the way we live to tell the truth about your love and your goodness. So we ask you to work in us and through us, to encourage us, and to lead us in your way. Thank you for your patience and for your grace. Amen.

SEVEN
CLARITY

They offer worship in a sanctuary that is a sketch and shadow of the heavenly one; for Moses, when he was about to erect the tent, was warned, "See that you make everything according to the pattern that was shown you on the mountain."

HEBREWS 8:5

The eye is the lamp of the body. So, if your eye is healthy, your whole body will be full of light; but if your eye is unhealthy, your whole body will be full of darkness. If then the light in you is darkness, how great is the darkness!

MATTHEW 6:22-23

Clarity: Insight, free from what obstructs, simplicity, transparency, enlightened, easily visible. Unhampered by restriction or limitation. To understand, freedom from ambiguity, certainty, comprehension.

One of the great sing-along hits of the early seventies was "I Can See Clearly Now," by Johnny Nash. Thirty years later, I can't read or hear the words without starting to hum along. Since its release the song has been covered by numerous artists so—regardless of whether we remember all of the lyrics—there's always someone in the car, the store, or (inevitably) the elevator who eventually belts out the refrain, "It's gonna be a bright (bright), bright (bright) sun-shiny day."

"Catchy song," one of my friends once told me, "but poor theology."

Freedom from Obstructions

> We look not at what can be seen but at what cannot be seen; for what can be seen is temporary, but what cannot be seen is eternal (2 Cor. 4:18).

One way the gift of faith helps us to see more clearly is by removing those obstructions that are liable to cloud our ability to see or to learn anything at all. How do we look at "what cannot be seen" unless we're willing to look with new eyes? And, while that's a nice turn of phrase, what does it mean, practically speaking, when we say those new eyes are actually the eyes of our hearts?

In the most basic terms, being able to see clearly is truly not such a great mystery. Rather than having to climb to the top of a spiritual mountain, what Paul means when he says we look "for what cannot be seen" involves more removing the blinders that inhibit our sight. The truth, it turns out, lies in realizing that "seeing God clearly" is not unnatural but is in fact the most natural thing in the world.

What's unnatural is the way we walk around with our eyes cast down or with blinders limiting our sight or with dark glasses obscuring our vision when what we need is to let the light flow in. What's unnatural is how we don't allow God to access our imaginations or to open our spiritual eyes so that we end up filtering what we see and hear through our presuppositions and not through God's. What's unnatural is our insistence that God conform to our personal, narrow-spirited nearsightedness, when what Jesus calls for is that we become willing to look up, to look beyond ourselves, and step purposefully into belief.

By living this way, we allow our arrogance and prejudice to have the (spiritual) gravitational pull of a black hole that sucks all imagination, wonder, creativity, and clarity of vision back into our own orbit. In effect, we can't see anything beyond the walls we have erected, the limited reasoning we employ, and the preconceptions and predeterminations we impose on both the people around us and the scope of our god (lower-case *g* intended).

We're like the man in Jesus' parable about the talents (Matt. 25:14-30). The master made an investment in some servants he believed in, but one servant buried what he'd been given because he had already concluded that his efforts would be futile. He didn't understand that the treasure was less the gold he was holding as what could be done with it. His actions became self-fulfilling, the negative outcome he predicted being predetermined by his elective blindness. His unwillingness to try to see beyond his own fears took the possibility of success or learning off the table.

When we fail in a similar manner, God, like the master in the parable, isn't as upset about the lost profit so much as the squandered opportunity. The greatest loss is not the interest or profit that might have been made but the lost opportunity for invention, imagination, creativity, and spirit. The greatest shortcoming is the inability to see and to believe.

To reiterate, poor vision leads to the loss of invention, imagination, creativity, and spirit.

A Theology of Mountains

The Appalachian Mountains are a favorite destination for vacation and retreat for my wife and me. There's a deep calmness to the topography that facilitates quiet and rejuvenation, prayer and contemplation, and spiritual and mental restoration. The mountains are also a great venue for photography.

One day we planned to drive the Blue Ridge Parkway south from Asheville, North Carolina. I looked forward to capturing some clear images of the scenic views. Unfortunately, our ascent to the ridge featured nothing but rain and clouds. My anticipation gave way to disappointment and I must admit that I became brooding and grumpy. I was so convinced we would miss out on the breathtaking views that I had been looking forward to that, pouting, I drove right past the first two scenic overlooks.

Thankfully my wife is consistently more clear-sighted than her ill-tempered husband. She wisely suggested that I pull over into the next overlook, get out of the car, and "just open your eyes."

I grudgingly took her advice and was soon amazed at what I saw. On that particular overcast day, thanks to the clouds and the gentle rain, I captured photos of a more nuanced Appalachia than I ever had before. Layers and depth appeared through the persistent drizzle that made it possible for me to appreciate the "blue" of the Blue Ridge. My eyes were, quite literally, opened.

That's when the realization hit me. It doesn't always need to be a "bright, bright, sun-shiny day." The fact is, we often see things in muted light that we miss in the stark contrast of bright sun and shadow. A clear day with dazzling sunlight can erase definition off the face of any scene. When that happens, we might just see a wash of light.

If we are honest with ourselves, what we see after overcoming our initial refusal to look can prove to be a blessing. God uses our eyes, our hearts, and our ability to observe to teach us more about the spiritual life.

Harvest Moon

Have you ever seen a huge harvest moon sitting low on the horizon? The orb hangs there front and center, seemingly suspended in midair, looking only a stepladder climb away—luminescent, orange and alive, like a glass ball owning its own soft light.

Or have you ever observed a sandhill crane float gently into the garden, landing like a 747 before walking across the grass with stately strides, each feather clear and crisp? Have you ever watched the ocean waves break onto the beach and swear you can see every molecule of water or break down every color like pouring out the contents of a kaleidoscope on a clean sheet of paper?

Have you ever seen something so intense that it causes you to wonder whether you have ever before seen anything in that kind of vivid detail?

What a curious thing. We can move beyond needing only reading glasses to requiring prescription lenses; or we may have difficulty hearing certain frequencies, and we can struggle to distinguish individual voices in a crowd. But then something happens in the realm of spiritual insight and we will swear we've never seen things this clearly before or we've never heard with the level of clarity that we do now.

"Do you still not perceive or understand?" Jesus asked. "Are your hearts hardened? Do you have eyes, and fail to see? Do you have ears, and fail to hear? And do you not remember?" (Mark 8:17-18).

Clarity is a life-charged word when we receive it as a spiritual gift: each morning an offering, every day an opportunity, every moment a step in increasing confidence, every relationship containing the seed of possibility.

A Shadow and a Copy

They serve at a sanctuary that is a copy and shadow of what is in heaven. This is why Moses was warned when he was about to build the tabernacle: "See to it that you make everything according to the pattern shown you on the mountain" (Heb. 8:5, NIV).

I like the way the NIV translation uses the words, "A copy and shadow of what is in heaven." When our vision becomes that clear, we can be sure that God is addressing us according to the "pay-close-attention" mode.

- Look!
- Listen!
- Finding clarity in the scripture; finding lucidity in the views; finding transparency in ourselves; finding meaning both in the books we read and in fellowship with one another; finding the Spirit in our praying.

God has so much to show us, and God continues to teach us even more. The Spirit urges each of us to "See to it that you make everything according to the pattern shown you on the mountain."

The life we are building always involves a journey, always requires commitment to forward movement, and always represents an epic work in progress. The phrase "A copy and a shadow of what is in heaven" may have referred to a physical structure designed for corporate worship, but the Bible also declares that our personal lives are a dwelling place for God. "Do you not know that your body is a temple of the Holy Spirit within you?" (1 Cor. 6:19).

God graciously gives us clarity, which provides a clear view of what is possible in the Spirit as we determine to engage in the life-charged life. The life that Christ lovingly and supportively leads us into is an echo, a mere a shadow and a copy, a sketch and shadow, of the deeper and more penetrating truth in heaven.

A Night at the Opera

- Check: Yes, this book is aimed at men.
- Check: Yes, a well-placed sports analogy, a hunting reference, a loud explosion, or a NASCAR illustration (in NASCAR you often get three out of four at one time . . .) will always help men's faith-based books along.
- But (check) there really is something for everyone here, and let's not forget that some guys do like opera too!

Well, a lot of guys don't like opera. And maybe you don't either. But most of us appreciate good music, creative artistry, and undeniable beauty even when presented in a form that's not necessarily our favorite.

Recently, I reluctantly accompanied my wife to the opera. The evening turned out OK, and I learned something about beauty and clarity. The experience made me think about C. S. Lewis's argument that the purest forms of beauty may actually be dangerous.

Lewis suggested that the beauty of heaven is so far removed from our earthbound experience and from the calibration of our human senses that it would destroy us if we were exposed to it. The idea that profound beauty can be described with words such as *withering* and *terrible* became a recurring theme in the way that the Oxford professor understood and talked about heaven.

Spiritual clarity can help us see more clearly what God is up to. It can also remove our blinders and help us to see beauty and purpose in our surroundings and in people we otherwise dismiss as unlovely or unworthy. Clarity can give us the eyes of Jesus and the responsibility to love that goes along with such clear-sightedness.

Remember how Moses needed to veil his face after spending time in the presence of God in order to protect the Israelites? In a similar sense, Lewis suggests that, as mortal human beings, we are not equipped to experience more than a hint, a suggestion, or a "shadow and a copy" of such dangerous splendor.

And so, because I'm a sports guy who doesn't like opera, the tabernacle-building metaphor from Hebrews helps explain what happened the evening my wife and I listened to a world-renowned soprano at Tampa's Performing Arts Center.

"The music was much more than a shadow and a copy," I wrote in my blog the next morning, "and the beauty of it almost killed me."

Life-charged clarity enriches our spiritual journey by showing us the "shadow and copy" of God's beauty. Sometimes, it feels as if the beauty is almost too much.

She Loves You (Yeah, Yeah, Yeah)

Some of us remember those tiny transistor radios that kids used back in the 1960s and 1970s. You may have listened to one of the "pirate" radio stations that broadcasted alternative music via weak AM signals from international waters off the coast of Europe or from across the border (in Mexico or Canada) or perhaps from some flimsy antenna in rural USA. The combination of the unreliable signal and inferior equipment would add up to a lot of static interspersed with vague phrases of music, along with a hint of the occasional series of words.

Hold that image. Now imagine sitting in an armchair, onstage, at a Beatles concert. John Lennon smiles at you as he strums his guitar. Paul McCartney stands a mere three feet away; you can see his fingers form the chords on the fret board of his bass guitar. George Harrison lays down a line of blues-edged rock so pure it makes your heart ache. And on the drums, right behind you, Ringo Starr taps the back of your chair.

The Fab Four follow up a bone-rattling rendition of "Revolution" with the classic anthem "Let It Be." They sing the harmonies in perfect pitch, and you do—you let it be. You let the sound wash over you. You feel the music.

Remember the transistor radio with the poor signal from a distant broadcast? Well, when compared to sitting onstage with John, Paul, George, and Ringo, that would be only "a copy and a shadow."

But let's make another shift: that live music experience (the Beatles onstage), so far and above listening to a song on a transistor radio, is itself merely "a copy and a shadow" of the beauty and the richness and the truth of the music we will experience in eternity. The distance from the live show to the reality of heaven is another exponential leap that we can't begin to understand.

We pattern our walk of faith, right now, on what we have been shown on the mountain. The richness and the beauty of life as a follower of Jesus makes the memory of our life outside of faith feel like "a copy and a shadow" compared to where we are now.

However, our current walk of faith is still just a shadow and a sketch of what is to come! As Fanny Crosby (1820–1915) wrote in her timeless hymn "Blessed Assurance," what we experience now is merely "a foretaste of glory divine."

You Don't Need Glasses When You Have Your Eyes Closed

As twenty-first-century Christian men, infusing our faith with real life requires clarity, even if it means seeing things we honestly don't want to see. But too often we're like the toddler who closes his eyes tight in the belief that "if I don't see it, then it isn't really there." Or we're like the man who bragged repeatedly to his friends about his cholesterol: "My score hasn't gone up a single point in twenty years." His secret? He never had it checked. Ironically, when he finally did have it checked again it was as a standard procedure for bypass surgery after his first heart attack.

> I pray that the God of our Lord Jesus Christ, the Father of glory, may give you a spirit of wisdom and revelation as you come to know him, so that, with the eyes of your heart enlightened, you may know what is the hope to which he has called you (Eph. 1:17-18).

Clarity Is a God Thing

> When [Elisha's servant] rose early in the morning and went out, an army with horses and chariots was all around the city. His servant said, 'Alas, master! What shall we do?' He replied, 'Do not be afraid, for there are more with us than there are with them.' Then Elisha prayed: 'O LORD, please open his

eyes that he may see.' So the LORD opened the eyes of the servant, and he saw; the mountain was full of horses and chariots of fire all around Elisha (2 Kings 6:15-17).

On occasion, spiritual clarity is purely a matter of opening our eyes. Always, clarity is a gift from God.

The Bottom Line (Open the Eyes of My Heart)

Here are some practical steps everyone can take to secure some life-charged clarity.

- More often than not, the best "next step" in any faith journey is to ask Jesus for help. "Lift the fog from my mind and spirit, Lord, because I am committed to seeing more clearly."
- Polish the lenses. Anyone who wears glasses knows that if you get caught up in life and forget to take care of them, they're going to make your vision foggier. When you do clean them it seems like a miracle! Here are a few effective ways to polish the lenses of our heart:
  - Pray, every day, all day. God knows how to make matters clear. In addition, there's a powerful response of the heart when you ask one or more friends to pray with or for you.
  - Read scripture. Has it been a few days since you last spent some time reading the Bible? If it's been more than twenty-four hours, then it's been too long.
  - Involve your community. There's nothing like bouncing ideas off a few Christian friends if you're looking for clarity. The Quakers call this a

"Clearance Session" and for good reason. The more time you spend with other people of faith, the more life-charged your sense of clarity will be.

- Attend worship. Regular worship is life-activating. How many times have you heard a friend say, "I'm not sure what it was about church today, but I can see things so much more clearly now"?

- Read faith-based resources. You can make your conversation about faith more constant and informed by having a good faith-based book (like this one) going at any given time.

- Listen to faith-based music. Try substituting some of your favorite spiritual artists for talk radio, or those nonstop telephone calls when you're on the road. It's amazing how much life-charged clarity seeps into your subconscious when you're tuned in to higher thoughts as a matter of routine.

Let's Talk about It

Use these questions for personal reflection, in reading this book with a couple of friends, or for discussion as a study group in your faith community.

1. Would you say you see more clearly at this stage of your life or less clearly? To what do you attribute the shift?

2. When Jesus talked about "having eyes to see," he was expressing frustration about those who do not have eyes to see. Name some of the "blinders" you think came between the people Jesus knew and clarity. Name some blinders that tend to keep you in the dark.

3. Share an experience when an event or a comment enabled you to see more clearly. How has that experience enriched your faith life?

4. In what way does your faith help you see more clearly?

5. For you, is it true that "seeing is believing" or that "believing is seeing"?

6. Think about the idea that some experiences are "a shadow and a copy" of spiritual or kingdom experiences. In what ways does that claim make sense to you?

PRAYER: Often, God, we ask that you open our eyes and help us see more clearly. Then, when you do, we hide from the truth you reveal. So we pray for the faith to see through spiritual eyes and the courage to allow what is revealed to change us, to help us grow, and to make us life-charged ambassadors of grace and justice and love and truth. Amen.

EIGHT
PRAYER and TRANSFORMATION

[Jesus] was praying in a certain place, and after he had finished, one of his disciples said to him, "Lord, teach us to pray."

LUKE 11:1

Prayer: A deliberate practice of interaction with God; the practice of addressing a divinity.

Transform: To change in character or condition; to alchemize, make over, metamorphose, transfigure, convert, transmute, transpose, transubstantiate.

Prayer in the morning is life-charged by definition. Morning prayer sets both context and direction for the coming hours. A man can pray any time of the day, but the power of morning prayer is that you have already invited God along for the ride.

After a recent talk, a man challenged my conviction that faith, life, relationships—in fact, nearly everything—can be "new every morning." He asked about it with an edge to his voice, the statement expressed almost as an accusation.

"You're always going on about morning devotions," he said in a slightly defensive tone. "Or about getting out of bed with an attitude of thanksgiving. Or bringing your wife a cup of tea or coffee before she gets up, so the first interaction you have is one of service and care. Why the big deal about what happens so early in the day?"

It didn't sound quite so bad the way he was telling it. But he wasn't finished.

"What I want to know is, what's wrong with reading the Bible at lunchtime? Why can't I pray on my way home from work? And where in the Bible does it say there's something second-rate about being nice to my wife after we've had dinner? Huh?"

Hard to argue with reasoning like that!

Trajectory of Intention

So let's kick this chapter off by responding to the objections. For starters, nothing is wrong with praying or reading your Bible or showing your wife a kindness at lunch or in the afternoon or anytime, and I don't mean to imply that. But what happens at the beginning of each day matters a great deal. Getting off to a good start is critically important to any project, not least the life-charged life. The way we launch the gift of a new morning sets a trajectory of intention, promise, and potential that is transformational not only for us as Christian men but also for the people we encounter during the day and the work we accomplish or the recreation we enjoy.

You are more likely to read the Bible at lunchtime if you have already been open to hearing God's Word since your day began. You are more likely to pray on your way home from work if you first prayed the moment your feet touched the floor on your side of the bed in the morning and continued to pray, at intervals, during the day. Men are exponentially more apt to treat their wives well both during and after dinner if they have first welcomed them into the new day with an act of service and love.

In other words, the impetus of what is to come grows out of those first few moments of the day with deliberation and power. It's possible that events along the way may have some impact. But once the course is set and God is invited into both our conscious and unconscious thoughts, the advantage is with faith.

Choose the Bearing and Calibrate the Trajectory

Our privileged, life-charged opportunity is to be men who choose our bearing, calibrate the trajectory, plan the route, and load the potentiality—rather than allowing ourselves to launch aimlessly into the unsympathetic buffeting of happenstance.

Transformational living depends in large part on our personal choice, a huge variable that happens to be under our control as men interested in experiencing the life-charged life. Here it is again, in handy bullet-point form. Our daily opportunity is to

- choose our bearing
- calibrate the trajectory
- plan the route
- load the potentiality

Men and Prayer

> Rejoice always, pray without ceasing, give thanks in all circumstances; for this is the will of God in Christ Jesus for you. Do not quench the Spirit (1 Thess. 5:16-19).

As a news writer and conference leader, I have been privileged to enjoy several years of deliberate faith-based conversation with a wide array of men, including in-depth interviews with over four hundred pastors; weekly small group sessions that have included more than one hundred different members over the span of twenty years; heart-to-heart discussions with many hundreds of participants at a variety of spiritual retreats and conferences; and extensive online dialogue in response to news articles, virtual classes, and blog posts concerning men's spirituality. The majority of these men (both those classified as "seekers" and those more deeply involved with church ministry) fall well short of the designation "thoroughly engaged" in an active prayer life.

So here's a good question: where would you say that you fit in when it comes to owning an approach to prayer that may or may not be classified as "life-charged"?

An Unscientific Assessment Scale

The following comprises an informal scale (read, *very* informal) to help you rate yourself and your approach to prayer. Put a check mark by each statement that is true in your experience. These questions are cumulative (meaning that a check alongside number 4 presupposes checks at numbers 1, 2, and 3 as well).

1. I pray at church, when I go, as a general participant.
2. Sometimes I'll say a blessing before meals.
3. Occasionally, especially in a sticky situation, I ask God to help me or maybe I recite the Lord's Prayer.
4. Once in a while, when God comes to mind, I will pause and offer a short prayer.
5. At least once a week or more, I have a brief "quiet time" dedicated to a few minutes of Bible reading and prayer.
6. I don't think a day goes by that I don't talk with God, for at least a couple of minutes or more, often more than once a day. The more I do this, the more I shut up and learn to listen.

7. I acknowledge God and turn to God several times every day. Often it turns into a few minutes of serious prayer. I find these times most meaningful when I've devoted at least five to ten minutes to a formal devotional time in the morning.

8. I believe I've crossed the threshold into the realm of "prayer without ceasing." Nearly everything in my life runs through the filter of my consciousness of God. Strange thing, I don't experience it as intrusive; God runs like a computer operating system, underneath and behind everything else.

We could nuance this conversation even more, but the eight descriptions of a prayer life listed above are enough for this basic discussion. Research suggests that very few men, Christian or otherwise, could make more than a tentative check mark beyond number five. Some of the rationalizations we hear for why we don't go further include these: "Well I'm just not that good at prayer." "Give me a work project. I like to serve God that way." "I feel stupid, like I'm talking to myself." "I wouldn't know what to say." "I'd pray more if I wasn't so busy." "I'm not sure that I want God up in every part of my business that much." Or, "I'm not a natural pray-er, like some people I know."

There are literally hundreds more explanations where those came from. But the most useful fact to glean from this part of the discussion is that taking time to pray is always our choice. Prayer is primarily about making the decision to put ourselves in a place where God is an interactive part of our conscious decision making. The more we do this, the more natural it will feel.

A Deeper Time with God

"Prayer is the soul's sincere desire, unuttered or expressed" (James Montgomery, 1771–1854).

From time to time a simple moment of prayer can lead into a deep time of communion with God. The key is to approach God with an open heart and a lack of obvious distractions.

Stephen opened his email one day and found a message from a member of his small group. "Please pray for us and our son," it read. "Details when we see you Sunday."

Stephen prayed accordingly and felt an unusual surge of connection with the Spirit. So he prayed beyond the standard, "God bless so-and-so." His prayer became an intimate interaction that worked its way into his conscious self and then penetrated deeper places he could not fathom. He found he couldn't pray for his friend's son in isolation, so he prayed for his daughter as well. Since each member of his small group had children, Stephen felt called to pray through every family in the circle. All in all, he prayed with care and with different emphases (depending on the individual) for ten married couples, one single person, and twenty-four young-adult children.

Deliberate Time

Spending deliberate time in prayer every morning will prevent the experience from becoming rote or repetitive, because an active relationship will emerge. Deliberate prayer begins to take the direction God wants it to take. On that particular day, Stephen's openness to the Spirit became a deep, serious conversation that lasted forty-five minutes and affected everything else about the balance of his day.

Our prayer becomes life-charged when we take the time to engage God on a regular basis and move beyond the perfunctory pleasantries. But it won't even begin to change until we have decided to be more deliberate and have taken steps to make it happen.

What Makes Prayer a Life-charged Word?

Prayer is, by its very nature, a conscious connection with the breathtaking, yet personal power that designed and created the universe. Prayer allows us to tap into the ultimate source of life. Plugging into God is not optional if we are serious about moving from the mundane and into the remarkable.

God is The Franchise when it comes to life.

It is of paramount importance that we understand prayer as interactive rather than merely some unthinking monologue we run inside our head. Prayer is an interaction that appreciates familiarity, demands respect, cannot afford to neglect listening, necessitates patience, benefits from regularity, improves with repetition, thrives on trust, grows with experience, and will ultimately flounder if we fail to allow it to lead to faith-based responses in terms of how we live.

Transformation

> Jesus said to her, "I am the resurrection and the life. Those who believe in me, even though they die, will live, and everyone who believes in me will never die. Do you believe this?" (John 11:25-26).

There's a fallacy that remains alive and well in this world that goes like this: "Humankind is constantly improving itself."

There was a time during the nineteenth century when the Age of Enlightenment began to bump into the Industrial Revolution, and scientific knowledge exploded. Many intelligent people (not just humanists and transcendentalists but Christians too) started talking about the progress of human knowledge and achievement. Some people became convinced that humankind was on the verge of eliminating disease, poverty, conflict, and more. We were going to improve ourselves right into peace and harmony and prosperity.

Well, right. Okay then. How's that working out? The twentieth and twenty-first centuries happened along; humankind not only continued fragmenting, fighting, and killing one another, but we also proceeded to do it at a record pace. So let's agree that transformation, as a purely evolutionary construct, may well have fallen short of the job of making us better people.

Religionized Christianity (or, to put it another way, Christianized religiosity) has also failed when it comes to moving us forward. Rather than leading the charge, mainstream and fundamentalist faith is too often identified with anti-change, intractability and reactionary stick-in-the-mud-ism, even though we claim to have a faith that's alive and we acknowledge that change is part of the definition of life.

Prayer: The Most Compelling Agent of Change

Change must be a foundational part of a prayer life that is life-charged. If we pray (and pray without ceasing) then God will accomplish transformational work in and through us. We can count on it. Prayer brings the kind of transformation this world desperately needs. Prayer brings the kind of transformation each of us so desperately needs.

Life-charged prayer (which means a prayer-life that consistently hovers around the six to eight range on the informal scale outlined earlier) is a transformative experience by definition.

Life = Change = Transformation

There are many definitions of life, but each of them boils down to the following elemental characteristics:

- Life is that which distinguishes what is vital and functional from what is dead.
- Life is a force associated with animation or vigor.
- Life is a state characterized by metabolism, growth, the ability to react, reproduction, and constant adaptation via internal change.

Visitors to Mount Saint Helens (the volcano in Washington state that erupted in spectacular fashion in 1980) can witness geological life right in front of their eyes. The mountain's ongoing vitality is evidenced in the new cone growing inside the huge crater.

A person can experience a similar sense of awareness at the rim of the Grand Canyon, looking down to the thin ribbon of silver that's the Colorado River, five thousand feet below. Running water and other elements of progressive weathering are still sculpting the details of one of the world's most massive features.

Power!

Both of these ongoing natural events make a humbling sight. A person cannot be in either location without considering the fact that God is still creating and recreating this world. That is the kind of power that resides in our decision to follow Jesus today and in our willingness to allow God the latitude to change us and act as a constant force for transformational life in our day-to-day routines.

Biologists report that part of the definition of life involves the ability to take in energy from the environment and to transform it for growth and reproduction. That process is also the difference between lip service and life-charged prayer. Life-charged prayer transforms us for spiritual growth and for reproduction. Because we are charged with life and, therefore, changing and reproducing, the world we inhabit is necessarily changed too. Sometimes that's a bit much for us to process.

The Bottom Line

"Okay," you might say. "I'm a man and I acknowledge that I need more transformational life in my prayer life. But how do I proceed from here? I'm a little nervous, but I'm also tired of being stuck in this surface-level relationship with God."

That's a great question, and one I address in the chapter titled "Community." But here are some starters.

- First, you're over halfway there if you accept *prayer* as one of your life-charged words. Desire is always the prelude to discipleship (see *Get Real: A Spiritual Journey for Men*, Upper Room Books, 2007). Prayer is not a formula but rather the exploration of a relationship. Like all relationships, our connection with God responds to consistency, care, and honest effort.
- Second, let's refer to the informal prayer scale (pages 118–119). Figure out what step on the list best describes you. Maybe you're all over the place. Now read question six: "I don't think a day goes by that I don't talk with God, for at least a couple of minutes or more, often more than once a day. The more I do this, the more I shut up and learn to listen." There is no expectation that anyone will become a spiritual giant overnight, but it is important to make the deliberate choice to cultivate an open heart.

- Third, find a daily devotional guide that you're comfortable reading. The *Upper Room* magazine is a great place to start, but there are a number of helpful options. Be sure to use the guide every morning, first thing. You'll find that when you begin the day with God, you naturally continue to pray throughout the day.
- Fourth, ask God to transform you (this should be a constant element of your daily prayer). Be both patient and persistent. God will show you the best place to begin. If life-charged prayer becomes your constant companion, then life, the insistent Christ-life, will have its way.

Let's Talk about It

Use these questions for personal reflection, in reading this book with a couple of friends, or for discussion as a study group in your faith community.

1. Did you grow up with prayer as a regular part of your home life? If not where did you first learn how to pray? If yes, how has that affected your lifelong practice of prayer?
2. In what ways are you nervous about involving God in the details of your life? Explain your answer, and why or why not you'd like your answer to change.
3. Read this passage in which Paul prays his heart out. Read it out loud, even if you are alone.

> For this reason I bow my knees before the Father, from whom every family in heaven and on earth takes its name. I pray that, according to the riches of his glory, he may grant that you may be strengthened in your inner being with power through his Spirit, and that Christ may dwell in your hearts through faith, as you

are being rooted and grounded in love. I pray that you may have the power to comprehend, with all the saints, what is the breadth and length and height and depth, and to know the love of Christ that surpasses knowledge, so that you may be filled with all the fullness of God. Now to him who by the power at work within us is able to accomplish abundantly far more than all we can ask or imagine, to him be glory in the church and in Christ Jesus to all generations, forever and ever. Amen (Eph. 3:14-21).

4. What does Paul say about transformation?
5. If you had three minutes dedicated to private time with God, how would you divide up that time? Design a basic pattern and then implement your plan, three times a day, for the coming week.
6. Who do you know who has an active and transformational prayer life? Consider picking that person's brain about what is working in his or her personal practice of prayer.
7. Do you believe doubt should stop you from praying? Why or why not? Where do you rank yourself on the "doubt-faith continuum" when it comes to prayer?

PRAYER: We invite you into our minds and our spirits, gracious God. We set aside our reservations and our doubts and declare that now is the acceptable time to step into a more active prayer life. We want to know that you are a vital part of everything we do, and we want you to know that we are committed to life-charged prayer. Amen.

NINE
AUTHENTICITY

[Gideon] responded, "But sir, how can I deliver Israel? My clan is the weakest in Manasseh, and I am the least in my family." The LORD said to him, "But I will be with you, and you shall strike down the Midianites, every one of them."

JUDGES 6:15-16

Authenticity: The quality of being actually and exactly what is claimed; trustworthy; authoritative. Worthy of acceptance or belief; genuine; not counterfeit.

Most men try their best to avoid clichés, but there's one cliché that guys probably appreciate when it's applied to them: "What you see is what you get."

We men like that. We like honesty. We appreciate the absence of game playing in relationships; we like frankness and truth. We'll forgive pretty much anything if someone steps up and admits to his or her failings, but falsity sticks in our craws.

Authenticity is a characteristic Jesus recognized and valued too. Listen to this passage from John:

> Nathanael said to him, "Can anything good come out of Nazareth?" Philip said to him, "Come and see." When Jesus saw Nathanael coming toward him, he said of him, "Here is truly an Israelite in whom there is no deceit!" (John 1:46-47).

A Rare Moment

In the biblical narrative, Jesus rarely breaks from the action at hand to throw out a compliment regarding someone he's never met before. But that is what he does with Philip's friend, Nathanael.

Nathanael is "a man's man" if ever there was one. Yes, that's a dated expression, possibly with chauvinistic overtones. But we know what it means. It means that Nathanael was a "what you see is what you get" kind of a guy. No pretense. No hidden agendas. No games. No prevarication, no fabrication, no pontification, no obfuscation. But, being the man he was, Nathanael probably wouldn't have used words like those. Jesus nailed his personality right on the head.

"Here is truly an Israelite in whom there is no deceit," Jesus commented to whoever might be listening. And deceit is guaranteed to suck life directly out of a man or relationship or, for that matter, an entire life—whether male or female.

If Nathanael was such a standout, I wonder what Jesus considered normal behavior from the other people he knew.

Handyman Special

Many of us have watched one of those the-pressure-is-on-to-sell-your-house cable shows. Several versions exist, involving everything from major remodeling to only a few bucks spent on creative staging. The idea is to help the homeowners by making the house look more attractive to the people who are looking to purchase.

Fair enough. New paint, clean carpets, and eliminating clutter help potential buyers see beyond the mess and evaluate the house on its merits. Landscaping works the same way. Cut back the bushes, add some flowering plants, fix the sidewalk, or replace dead areas and weeds with new sod. Realtors describe this as "curb appeal."

One recent episode featured a fix-it team discussing whether to resod the yard. The work was listed as a priority for "moving" the house. But instead of bringing in sod, they decided to spray-paint the dead grass and weeds so they could save funds for other projects. No kidding! Halfway through the episode, a truck rolled up with a tank and a hose and the guy applied dye to the entire yard. He was done in fifteen minutes but hung around to talk with the hosts.

"I'm making a good living here in Florida," the contractor said. "My clients are mostly distress sales—banks and realtors who don't want to waste money on landscaping. So they have me come by with my truck. It helps the home show better, you know."

Surprisingly, everyone seemed okay with this. There were no ethics-based questions by the hosts; no hesitation from the homeowners; and no, "Now wait a minute?" from the realtor evaluating the project.

"I'm impressed," the show hosts said. "Now this looks like healthy grass. At first glance buyers will never know the difference."

Talk about blatant manipulation. What bothered me more than the deception was the fact that nobody seemed to mind. To them the charade was legitimate because appearance is the name of the game.

When appearance is the name of the game, then what you see is most certainly not what you get. Rather than life-charged, inauthentic is always life draining.

False Front

Last year I scheduled an interview with a preacher for a newspaper story I was writing. His church Web site popped up during my online research for background facts; it was loaded with information. I took a few notes, turned off my computer, jumped into my car, and headed to the nearby town with the impression that the man I was scheduled to visit was the senior pastor at an active, five-hundred-plus-member congregation with multiple staff, expansive facilities, cutting-edge programs, and an emergent worship style led by a praise team so dynamic it was on the verge of landing its first big recording contract with a Nashville music label.

The address wasn't familiar, so I let the GPS guide me. It wasn't long before I found myself in a residential neighborhood, and when I pulled up at the church "office" I realized the congregation met in a small family home.

I rang the doorbell. The preacher let me in and we chatted about his life and ministry. It turned out he's a full-time salesman who'd been fired from three consecutive assistant-pastor positions before deciding to start a new church by himself.

A few questions revealed that the church Web site featured stock photographs of people completely unrepresentative of his small flock, worship images lifted from some other church's home page, and pictures of buildings not even located in the state of Florida. The site presented a picture of a congregation that no one had ever experienced.

Most Sundays nine people attended worship service, Preacher Pete told me. His wife and three children accounted for four. "But we've had as many as twelve," he said.

So I asked him about the church's Web site. "Web pages are considered the front lobby of a church today," I said. "Don't you think the picture you're painting should be more authentic?"

"But I have a tremendous vision for this program," he said.

And so do the people who sell those exercise bikes to middle-aged men using twenty-year-old professional models with perfect bodies, I thought.

The Real Thing!

There is absolutely no substitute for reality. Authenticity appeals far more than any fakery designed merely to sell. Authenticity adds life; fakery takes life away. Incomplete or contrived information is damaging in the world of faith too. The inauthentic wreaks havoc in relationships, in institutions, in the presentation of the gospel, in testimonials, and in personal faith. When appearance trumps authenticity, on occasion it may look as if there's a temporary gain, but in the long run everyone loses.

Hiding behind a Façade

We live in a culture that so values appearance that it often becomes difficult to ascertain what is real based solely on what we see. I'm reminded of the many storefronts built with façades, which suggest a spacious three-story showroom when the building is in fact very different. Plastic surgery is performed at epidemic levels, even among teens. People purchase cars, houses, clothes, and other items that they can't afford because personal value has been linked to possessions. People create false online identities to initiate relationships based on attributes they don't actually possess. Résumés are tweaked in order to gain access to a job or some other opportunity. Sales programs are designed to lure people "in the door" via blatant deceit.

Lifeless Plastic

Contrary to popular belief (and most advertising), authenticity is not a liability. I suspect that most of us trust people who present themselves at face value and without prevarication more than those who put on a false front. Trust is a huge element in making connections, and in the long run reliability wins over flashy every time.

Unfortunately, in spite of our cumulative common sense, many of us still build significant elements of our lives on lies and deceit. A leading cable news program recently aired a segment on "The Finances of Dating." Apparently, in order to make a strong first impression, some men will take a date to a restaurant they can't afford, adding to an already tenuous credit balance. But once the precedent has been set, they are likely to repeat the performance the next time. The result is that relationships develop predicated on misrepresentation and false expectations.

Think of the irony that credit is accessed with cards often described as "plastic." The word *plastic* is universally accepted as a euphemism for inorganic, lifeless, false, or artificial.

Danger, Danger!

As we consider what it means to add life-charged authenticity to the way that we live, we occasionally find it difficult to break away from the pretenses that define so much of day-to-day life.

- Do we have the confidence to reject false standards of manliness, to risk vulnerability, and to build authentic relationships?
- Can we abandon our culture's acquisition-based definition of success, even as we understand that the pursuit of material wealth will never satisfy?
- Are we afraid to dismantle our façades to avoid admitting we've wasted so much time and effort for so many years?
- Can we develop the humility necessary to invite and to accept Jesus as Lord in our lives?
- Are we ready to open our hearts, lay our souls bare, jettison the games and own up to the depths of our pain, and allow God to heal us from the need to look anything other than grateful and redeemed?

Truth Is a Powerful Witness

Living the life-charged life but not walking in the truth proves nearly impossible. This principle is seldom illustrated so clearly as when we talk about our spiritual journey, especially with nonbelievers.

Remember the part of the definition of life that states, "Authentic life replicates itself naturally"? Well, when we communicate a faith story that is obviously exaggerated or patently disingenuous or not borne out in experience, then replication most certainly becomes an issue. There's no life to falsity. For faith to be life-charged, we need genuineness or our story falls flat.

We've heard reports about skeptics, agnostics, and even atheists who are won over to faith because the Christian person they ran into was genuine. In the end, fine arguments or intellectual acumen or force of personality will not tell the story of God's love; but people living faithfully, without pretense, and letting the light and the life of authenticity speak beyond the words can tell that story.

Life, authentic life, speaks for itself.

How to Be Authentic

The answer is a no-brainer. Just tell the truth. But the *process* requires a little more than that.

First, we have to know ourselves. We can't live authentically if we let our culture, our friends, the media, or any other outside "authority" define who we're supposed to be and force us to play the role. The psalmist did most of his introspection in the presence of God:

> O LORD, you have searched me and known me. You know when I sit down and when I rise up; you discern my thoughts from far away. You search out my path and my lying down, and are acquainted with all my ways. Even before a word is on my tongue, O LORD, you know it completely. . . . Search me, O God, and know my heart; test me and know my thoughts (Psalm 139:1-4, 23).

Jesus was crystal clear regarding his identity. When faced with the hostility of some religious leaders, he made them even more unhappy by saying, "Very truly, I tell you, before Abraham was, I am"

(John 8:58). That's a level of self-knowing that cannot be achieved outside a deep and regular discipline of life-charged prayer.

Second, we must be as honest about admitting our doubts as we are about affirming our assurances. When we allow ourselves to engage in honest struggle, when we let God in on the conversation about uncertainty, and when we are not afraid to share the complete picture with others, then we have created room for faith. Faith without honesty is not faith at all.

Third, we need to step up and claim the light that we have been given. Sometimes our experience of God may be as a sliver of daylight shining through an otherwise closed window or the hint of a breeze blowing through a slightly cracked door. If we acknowledge our doubts then we must be equally forthcoming when it comes to our experiences of grace.

This is what testimony is about. We affirm the light that we have, even when that light doesn't give us a lot to hold onto. Surprisingly, in that affirmation a curious thing happens, like driving a wedge into the crack from where the light is coming and opening up a flood. When we humbly share and affirm our experience of God, however small, we are given more assurance to share. Confidence builds on confidence.

The Bottom Line

Faith possesses us with reassuring life when we stop trying to tie down tidy answers. Authenticity is life-charged inasmuch as it requires that we deal plainly with God. Authenticity would have had Adam come out from hiding among the trees into the presence of God with the apple core in his hand to save the relationship.

> They heard the sound of the LORD God walking in the garden
> at the time of the evening breeze, and the man and his wife

hid themselves from the presence of the LORD God among the trees of the garden (Gen. 3:12).

- God wants the man who wakes up in the morning with questions and doubts, yet who reads his Bible and prays anyway.
- God wants the man who is flawed and selfish and now and then a little lazy, yet who sees himself as a disciple moving along the road with purpose.
- God wants the man who is concerned about his finances, yet who practices generosity.
- God wants the man who fails in terms of sainthood, yet who asks for forgiveness and carries on.
- God wants the man who knows too well that he is not a model of piety, yet who stands up and testifies to the goodness and grace of God whenever the opportunity arises.

We are pilgrims on the road; the most convincing story we have to share is the story of our own struggle and the faithfulness of God in response.

Let's Talk about It

Use these questions for personal reflection, in reading this book with a couple of friends, or for discussion as a study group in your faith community.

1. Why do you think so many Christians misrepresent themselves?
2. What message do the following environments communicate to you about expressing questions, doubts, and struggles in your life:

- church
- work
- friends
- family
- God
- yourself

3. Whom do you know that you can be 100 percent honest with? If you cannot name anyone, explain why you think that is.

4. Why do you think confessing your doubt is as important as confessing your belief?

5. What makes the truth such a powerful witness?

PRAYER: Lord, we can't deny that being honest about our struggles with faith makes us stronger. Yet we find it difficult to own up to our doubts and failures. Help us become more like the man who told Jesus that he believed and then asked for help with his unbelief. We understand that you are always willing to meet us where we are, but we find it difficult to acknowledge where that place is. Help our confusion and be gracious to us as we continue this pilgrimage of life. Amen.

TEN
COMMUNITY

Two are better than one, because they have a good reward for their toil. For if they fall, one will lift up the other; but woe to one who is alone and falls and does not have another to help . . . A threefold cord is not quickly broken.

ECCLESIASTES 4:9-10, 12

Community: Owning certain interests in common; common ownership or participation; in biology, organisms in a community affect one another's profusion, distribution, and adaptation.

Koinonia: Community, communion, participation together; sharing, closeness, knowing and intimacy.

Conrad is an active officer in the United States Marine Corps. He's tough, he's decorated, he lives a life of meaningful discipleship, and he loves his community of faith. One day Conrad was discussing the tendency of the military culture to discourage servicemen and servicewomen from looking for help when they run into the need for emotional support.

"The higher brass put out a memo," he said. "It instructed the officers to attend sensitivity training so we'd be better equipped to deal creatively with the increase in suicide in the ranks."

Conrad shook his head, disturbed, as if he still couldn't believe what had happened. "When we showed up for training, we didn't need our notebooks and there wasn't any group discussion. We didn't even need that much time.

"'Get in their faces and tell them to shape up,' we were told. 'Tell them they're Marines and remind them that Marines suck it up. Tell them the Marine Corps isn't for babies and if they're not happy they need to get over it in a hurry. They'd better not come crying to us.'"

That was it. "Supportive Community 101." End of story.

Granted, the dynamic Conrad described is very much old school. Many military commands are open to change and are willing to address problems of stress, loneliness, and depression. But my friend's experience is more than a commentary on the armed services; it's a commentary on what it means to be a man in North America—a pervasive maladaptation men as a group must strive to go beyond if we are to experience life in its fullness.

Paradox

A strange paradox exists in the life of men. On the one hand, our culture sends the message that rugged individualism and self-sufficiency are lauded values (and nearly as valued as a religion); that asking for assistance is against "the man code"; that real men don't show emotions, and they ration their words. In fact, in many professions, men who seek counseling with any kind of mental health professional risk it being a career-ending decision.

On the other hand, and at the same time as we hold the sentiments mentioned above, we seem to agree about the value of groupthink and team play. For many men the memory of being a member of a sports team in their youth is a highlight that is seldom matched in adulthood. Effective military units operate as a close-knit "band of brothers." Solitary confinement is considered one of the most potent forms of abuse, and extreme isolation is a danger sign that involves not only relationships but also mental health in general.

In the face of this mixed message, many men choose isolation over community, time and again. And the same work culture that recognizes the value of transparency and teamwork discourages (at times not so subtly) those who seek help, even when it is needed the most.

Many of us know or are aware of husbands who have chosen to shut themselves down emotionally rather than to confide in their wives. Many of us have friends who keep issues at a distance. And many of us know or have heard about neighbors who never reveal a glimpse of the pain and the turmoil they're hiding inside.

As a gender, men often deal with stress by pretending it isn't there, building walls around their psyche for fear of revealing their vulnerabilities. As a result, we consistently fail to acknowledge directly and openly our innermost selves, even to ourselves. And we neatly skirt around the slightest possibility of investing our authentic, unvarnished selves in other people. In doing so, we cut one another off from perhaps the most potent resource available.

And the community of men is impoverished.

No Free-pass for Christians

Even in faith-based communities (or, maybe, *especially* in faith-based communities), men take these widely accepted, community-oriented principles, park them in a seldom-plumbed recess of the brain, and proceed to avoid vulnerability, community, and accountability. In their place we substitute shallow conversations and "back-slapping" relationships with other men that go about as deep as this week's issue of *Sports Illustrated* or a show on ESPN.

Whatever the venue—church, marriage, work, recreation—literally millions of men routinely allow one of the most life-charged avenues at our disposal to become dumbed down to the level of sports talk around the cooler or high-fives and chest-bumps during the football season.

Got Your Back, Dude (Holding up One Another's Arms)

One of my favorite stories about community takes place in the book of Exodus, chapter 17. The narrative starts out with a verse that puts this entire conversation in context: "From the wilderness of Sin the whole congregation of the Israelites journeyed by stages, as the LORD commanded" (v. 1).

Moses and the Israelites were moving forward into the promise of their future. They were also leaving the wilderness, which ironically—in its English transliteration—captured the nature of their actions there. Almost immediately, before they had much of a chance to do anything other than quarrel and complain, they found themselves under attack by a king named Amalek (v. 8). Moses, realizing he could not handle the situation alone, sent Joshua to lead the Israelite troops and with Aaron and Hur climbed a hill to watch the battle. Then the most amazing thing happens. Listen to the story:

> Whenever Moses held up his hand, Israel prevailed; and whenever he lowered his hand, Amalek prevailed. But Moses' hands grew weary; so they took a stone and put it under him, and he sat on it. Aaron and Hur held up his hands, one on one side, and the other on the other side; so his hands were steady until the sun set. And Joshua defeated Amalek and his people with the sword (Exod. 17:11-13).

According to the story, Moses needed his friends by his side to share his burden. Moses needed community to hold his arms up.

That seems to cut against our preconceptions about Moses and about rugged individualism. Moses needed other guys? But he had God on his side, didn't he? We envision him, like Charlton Heston, with his staff (the one he used to perform miracles in front of Pharaoh while demanding "Let my people go!"). And now he has an army led by the mighty Joshua.

Do the math: Moses, plus God, plus a super-cool staff, plus the status, plus his sidekick Joshua? Really, didn't Moses already have enough resources to handle this situation on his own?

The answer, of course, is no. The lesson is that we are not created to live as if we are self-sufficient. We are designed to function optimally in relationship with others. And this book is about what it means to function optimally.

We were created to live in community. That means a real, living relationship with God and with one another. Community is not optional when it comes to living the life-charged life.

So here's a question, guys: whom can you count on to help hold your arms up?

Self-sufficiency

The idea that men should be self-sufficient runs deep in our culture. Unfortunately, this dynamic frequently plays out in the male psyche as a stumbling block that too easily translates into a stridently anticommunity value. So ideas like "sharing," "won't you be my neighbor," "supporting one another," or anything that hints at revealing "need" or interdependence are difficult for men to accept.

And yet much (perhaps most) substantive personal and spiritual growth occurs in the context of small groups and honest relationships. *Community* is a life-charged word because it is exactly where we must be rooted if we are to fully engage the potential men have for dynamic, life-charged faith.

Community can be our ground zero for learning, our place of healing, our strong rock where we can anchor ourselves for stability, and our springboard for action.

Quiz Time

Does this sound like anyone you know? Around lunchtime at the office a call comes in. Philip answers, listens, nods a few times and then nervously hangs up the phone. It's the district manager. He wants Philip and his boss in the manager's office at day's end to talk about "some problems with the numbers, the issue of bad projections, and a few other concerns."

Philip doesn't feel good about this, and a cold sweat breaks out on his forehead.

So here's the question. If you were in this situation, how many men could you call and ask to pray *with* you or *for* you in the time between now and the meeting? Do you have guys who are familiar with your concerns, guys you could possibly pray with on the telephone, guys who might be willing to drop everything and meet with you for lunch or a quick coffee? Guys to help hold your arms up?

How many names could you come up with? One? Five? Ten? Zero? (Your pastor only counts if you included other guys as well.)

What if your wife called to say she's on the way to the hospital with one of your kids? Are there any men you could contact immediately, guys you could count on to listen, to reassure you that they're going to pray, to murmur encouragement, or to listen to you cry?

A True Story

Brian was a divorced, church-going man in his mid-thirties who insisted he had real friends. Sometimes he and "the guys" would hang out on Monday nights to watch football. They often spent several nights a week together playing on their congregation's softball team. On Sundays, when they ran into one another before or after worship, their conversations included things like, "Can you believe what happened in the game yesterday [baseball, college football, basketball]?" Then someone would say, "No way!" "It was wicked!" or "Who do you like for this afternoon's match up?" Then they'd laugh, commiserate about a mutual loss, "fist-bump," and go home.

Brian's dad had been sick for a number of months, and his condition was getting worse. Cancer. From time to time Brian would drive the three-hundred-mile round trip on a Saturday, but he'd catch enough sports on the radio or the Internet to converse intelligently Sunday mornings or catch up at the softball game. This went on for over six months until, finally, the cancer became critical, and Brian's dad went into hospice care.

Consequently, Brian missed several consecutive Sundays. When he managed to attend church, he'd pick up the same sports conversations with the guys he ran into in the lobby or around the coffeepot. One Wednesday evening, his dad died. Brian was devastated. He broke down and cried. Then he went to sleep. But he still didn't let anyone know.

The next morning Brian drove the one-hundred fifty miles to take care of arrangements. He took a long weekend, stayed over for the funeral Monday, and was back with the softball team for a game on Tuesday evening. He grounded out twice, was out on a pop fly in the fifth inning, then hit a double and scored late in the seventh inning.

"You looked pretty ragged out there for a while," one of his friends said after the game. "We didn't think you'd get a hit tonight. Is everything okay?"

Brian swallowed the lump in his throat, and briefly considered sharing the news about his dad, but then changed his mind because he didn't know if he could talk without letting his real feelings out. What if he broke down? What if he cried? Frankly, it felt like too big a risk. So he made some lame excuse about getting over a cold, punched his closest friend on the arm, climbed into his car and went back home.

Where Else Can a Man Go?

For me, writing a book often involves conversations with people who have a great deal of wisdom and insight about the subject at hand. One day, right in the middle of putting together these thoughts about life-charged community, I spent forty-five minutes chatting with the planning team for a Disciples of Christ men's conference in Bethany, West Virginia.

Pastor Greg Ott shared a conversation with me that he'd had with a professional counselor. They had been talking about men and the tendency of guys to live in a community-free vacuum. Men, in their typical daily routines, don't engage in the kind of heart-to-heart conversations that lead to the building of a life-charged community. When Greg mentioned the importance of small-group ministry in the local church, the counselor pointed out that in today's society, the church is possibly the only place where men can engage in these kinds of conversations. The church also may be the only place available where men can explore relationships that are defined by the levels of trust, honesty, confidence, and intimacy that we so desperately need.

Trust. Honesty. Confidence. Intimacy.

The experience of transformational community requires certain conditions for it to be truly life-charged: trust, confidentiality, honesty, vulnerability; a willingness to listen, the absence of judgment; love, commitment, intimacy, accessibility; faithfulness.

Life-charged community is not stagnant. It goes the extra mile; it makes an effort; it builds on those connections between scheduled meetings; and it reaches out, gives, receives, nurtures.

Question: Is This for Me? Answer: Yes!

Back to the question we posed earlier in this chapter: "Do you have any 'closer than a brother' friends?" Well, it turns out it doesn't matter if we are naturals at friendship or if we're actually better suited to retreating into our shell. Either way, the fact remains that all men—Christian or not—need to establish and maintain the kinds of connections we're talking about. Just because something requires more effort from some guys than others doesn't negate the value of the principle in question!

The man who says, "I'm not any good at making friends" is no more and no less in need of life-charged community than the one who has accumulated a dozen friends without even trying. We were created for relationship with God and we were created for relationship with other people. Building community is absolutely essential for any man who wants to engage his full potential.

This conversation does not involve personal strength or the ability to "tough it out" or to "man up" or to "suck it up." The man who distances himself from deep, openhearted, loving relationships with other men, by definition has compromised himself in terms of the life-charged life.

Glimpses

While the church is probably the one place where men can go to explore full-on, life-charged *koinonia*, it would be wrong and perhaps arrogant to suggest that the community of faith owns the franchise when it comes to practicing community. It remains possible to experience some level of community without being a follower of the Way. And there's good reason for this: God created every one of us, and God has packed each unique individual with life-charged potential. We have the promise because God designed us that way.

For example, the camaraderie of shared experience in a sports team is very real but only to an extent. Sports team meetings rarely include prayer or shared struggles with faith or the freedom to reveal fears and insecurities below the carefully presented surface of our psyches. Sports teams can't begin to replicate what becomes possible in a dynamic community of faith. The body of believers provides the best possible context to explore everything that *koinonia* can mean.

I once attended an international soccer game in London's Wembley Stadium. Over one hundred thousand people crowded together. There's an unofficial catalogue of a dozen or so anthem like songs that UK soccer crowds often spontaneously sing at big games, sometimes in fragments and sometimes complete. We sang "Land of Hope and Glory" and "You'll Never Walk Alone," and I felt the tears streaming down my face. The experience of community was genuine. The moment was truly spiritual, but it only went so far. I couldn't tap the guy in front of me on the shoulder, ask for his phone number, and call him for support later that week if I was feeling down and in need of prayer.

A lot of men have similar encounters at church, failing to connect, fearful of extending the opportunity for community beyond worship in the sanctuary, and immediately falling into more shallow patterns of relationship the moment they run into their friends in the lobby or out in the parking lot.

We All Have This Yearning to Bond

Many experiences provide glimpses into our need for and the promise of community. We bond with people when we're thrown together in dangerous circumstances, at concerts, during emotional sports events, or in the aftermath of tragic events. Why? Because God, who knows exactly what we need in order to experience the fullness of life, created us to connect with others at a deep level.

The need for community is built into our DNA. So why do we avoid deeper encounters in the context of our faith life? God is the one who created us this way; we are formed from God's imagination and purpose, created specifically for the practice of such a life-charged word.

The Bottom Line

Many of us have a barrier of pride, a pattern of expectation or resistance that we find challenging to move beyond after so many years and such an investment of self.

But, as scripture clearly illustrates, we must be prepared to engage the following question:

> If with Christ you died to the elemental spirits of the universe, why do you live as if you still belonged to the world? Why do you submit to regulations? (Col. 2:20).

This question confronts us with the need to decide if we want the word *community* to become a transformational, life-charged concept in our faith journey. We must decide to place ourselves in situations where we learn both to share and to receive, to associate with people who share our values and goals, and to communicate at a level that goes beyond the limitations of the ordinary.

Bottom Line points and recommendations:

- Jesus surrounded himself with a small group of men for prayer, support, and encouragement.
- Christianity is best as a team sport.
- You + a handful of other committed men + a God who believes in you = the same quality of life-charged community that revolutionized this world.
- Invest yourself in friendship with other men:
    - Invite a couple of the guys out to breakfast.
    - Share this book with a friend, and go through the questions together.
    - Share some prayer concerns.
    - Make yourself vulnerable.
- Join or start a men's ministry.

- Become part of a small group (covenant group).
- Start a support and accountability group with three to five men and pray for one another's families.

How this building block of your spiritual journey develops depends on a great many factors. However, whatever happens, understanding that community is not a disposable element or a take-it-or-leave-it "add-on" remains important. The decision to invest ourselves in vital community is probably one of the most critical steps we can take in the life-charged process.

Let's Talk about It

Use these questions for personal reflection, in reading this book with a couple of friends, or for discussion as a study group in your faith community.

1. Who are your best friends? What kind of things are you comfortable sharing (and not sharing) with them?
2. Why do you think Jesus placed himself in a tight-knit community? Of what value was this covenant community of men to Jesus?
3. Share (or write down) the names of two more guys with whom you may have the potential to develop a closer relationship and whom you'd like to know on a deeper level.
4. If you do decide to become part of a small community, what about your life would you rather the members not know or would you hold back? If there is something, where will you go if you need prayer and support and encouragement for that hidden aspect?
5. In John's Gospel, Jesus prayed,

I ask not only on behalf of these [disciples], but also on behalf of those who will believe in me through their word, that they may all be one. As you, Father, are in me and I am in you, may they also be in us, so that the world may believe that you have sent me (John 17:20-21).

    a. How do you think the community you are a part of is doing with regard to "all being one"?

    b. What do you believe Jesus is calling you to be involved with in terms of life-charged community?

6. Pray for the men in your church, your neighborhood, and your other circles of activity. Ask God to help you form a life-charged community. Be prepared to become a leader in whatever God prompts you to do.

PRAYER: Gracious God, you created each of us and filled us with life-charged potential. Help us to understand our need for *koinonia*. Surround us, we pray, with others who realize the importance of life-charged community. Fill us with the grace of expectation. Thank you. Amen.

BRINGING IT ALL TOGETHER (LETTING LIFE LOOSE)

In 2011 I launched my blog, "The Life-Charged Life" (derekmaul. wordpress.com). The purpose was (and remains) twofold: to explore the ideas that became the heart and soul of this book; and to invite my growing cadre of readers to participate in a vibrant, life-charged life.

Writer and philosopher Henry David Thoreau (1817–62) believed that most people fail to embrace life in all of its fullness. He made the troubling observation, "The mass of men lead lives of quiet desperation. What is called resignation is confirmed desperation" (*Walden*, 1854).

Thoreau's contemporary, Oliver Wendell Holmes (1809–94), expressed a related sentiment in his poem, "The Voiceless" (1858): "Alas for those that never sing, but die with all their music in them!"

10 Life-Charged Words attempts to put an end to such sad resignation that avoids the challenge to live as if we mean it. The ideas discussed in these ten chapters represent a life defined by fullness. Life-charged men are men who let their song find its voice. Or expressed in another way, the content of this book concerns the process of letting life loose.

The incidence of desperation observed by Thoreau and Holmes has become a huge issue in our severely fractured world, a quality that's often noticeable. When people fail to live according to the blueprint of their design, they experience frustration, angst, depression, dissatisfaction, anxiety, and desperation.

The way that Christians live tells the truth about the gospel they profess to believe. The word *gospel* supposedly means "good news." The sad truth is that too many men (and women) describe themselves as Christian but present the world with a model that can hardly be classified as good news at all. Rather than representing "the life that is truly life," what's often broadcast is not only tuneless but more along the lines of "the life that is barely a notch or two above desperate."

Hungry for Life-charged Good News

Our world is hungry for good news! One reason the words Jesus spoke (and the work that he did) continue to resonate through the ages is the fact that Jesus was basically brimming with vibrant life.

Life! Not gloom and doom and a new list of rules; not a holier-than-thou attitude; not self-righteousness. Instead, the gospel message is the story of irrepressible life. These 10 life-charged words represent the evidence of good news folded into the very fabric of our lives.

Our opportunity and our responsibility as followers of Jesus is to live in such a way that light and life spill out from us from the moment we wake up every morning and invite Jesus to live through us. Homes, neighborhoods, and workplaces are transformed because we are not afraid to claim a living relationship with Jesus. Everything we touch is improved as we practice an excellence motivated by our commitment to embrace the possibilities of the life-charged life. Relationships and faith communities become animated by our passion for the life that really is life. Creativity and productivity are enhanced as we redefine what it means to live at and beyond capacity. Promises are fulfilled, lives redirected, and spirits healed as scripture becomes the fuel for a renewed mind. Jesus' followers are empowered as leaders and equipped as healers via the beauty of holiness. We have newfound clarity of purpose as we pray for God to "Open the eyes of my heart, Lord." Prayer becomes integrated into the essential architecture of our personal operating system; trust is recreated and doubts conquered in response to a what-you-see-is-what-you- get authenticity that tells the truth about the gospel, basically by the way that we live. We develop communities of faithful men who are unafraid to be vulnerable, willing to be accountable, and motivated to be encouragers in their ongoing journey of discipleship as genuine followers of the Way of Jesus.

Each of us, as life-charged followers of Christ, tell the truth about the gospel of love simply by being and take a firm hold of "the life that is truly life."

In love, and because of love—DEREK

ABOUT THE AUTHOR

Award-winning journalist Derek Maul writes for magazines, newspapers, and online venues, including Guideposts, Newsweek, USA Today, and Chicken Soup for the Soul. Derek divides his time between writing and traveling to speak about the fully engaged Christian life. He is author of *Get Real* and *The Unmaking of a Part-Time Christian* as well as a book for Christmas, *In My Heart I Carry A Star*, and one for Easter, *Reaching Toward Easter*.

Derek lives near Tampa, Florida, with his wife, Rebekah. Learn more about Derek at www.derekmaul.com.